REBEC(
THE
SCREENPLAY

REBECCA

the
Screenplay
by
Arthur Hopcraft

*From the novel by
Daphne du Maurier*

Chameleon

First published in Great Britain in 1996 by
Chameleon Books
106 Great Russell Street
London WC1B 3LJ

Rebecca is a Portman production for Carlton UK
Television in association with WGBH/Boston
and Tele-münchen. © Carlton UK Television Limited
MCMXCVI.

Script text © Carlton UK Television Ltd
Photographs © Carlton UK Television Ltd

CIP data for this title is available from the British Library

ISBN 0 233 99055 0

Printed in Great Britain by
WBC, Bridgend

CAST LIST

Character	Artiste
Maxim de Winter	Charles Dance
Mrs. Danvers	Diana Rigg
Daphne	Emilia Fox
Mrs. Van Hopper	Faye Dunaway
Favell	Jonathan Cake
Crawley	Tom Chadbon
Beatrice	Geraldine James
Giles	Denis Lill
Granny de Winter	Jean Anderson
Colonel Julyan	Anthony Bate
Rebecca	Lucy Cohu
Frith	John Horsley
Robert	Jonathan Stokes
Ben	John Branwell
Tabb	Robin Soans
Coroner	Ian McDiarmid
Dr. Baker	Timothy West
Harbourmaster	Patrick Romer
Oldest Gardener	Frank Doherty
Hairdresser	Carla Mendonca
Nurse	Wendy Macadam
Clarice	Kelly Reilly
Nelson	David Webb
Tudor Lady	Zulema Dene
Napoleon	Michael Wynne

PRODUCTION TEAM

Executive Producers	Jonathan Powell
	Tim Buxton
Producer	Hilary Heath
Co-Producer	Andrew Warren
Director	Jim O'Brien
Executive Producer for WGBH	Rebecca Eaton
Executive Producer for Tele-münchen	Rikolt Von Gagern
Associate Producers	Steve Matthews
	George Adams
Screenplay by	Arthur Hopcraft
Director of Photography	Rex Maidment B.S.C.
Production Designer	Caroline Amies
Editor	Michael Parker
Sound Recordist	Peter Sutton
Costume Designer	Elizabeth Waller
Script Editor	Steve Matthews
Casting Director	Doreen Jones
Music composed by	Christopher Gunning
Consultant for the Du Maurier Estate	Robin Lowe
Production Manager – France	Frederic Bovis
1st Assistant Director	Nick Heckstall-Smith

2nd Assistant Director	Jamie Christopher
3rd Assistant Director	Zerlina Hughes
Production Co-ordinator	Nathalie Tanner
Location Manager	Mark Mostyn
Unit Manager	John Bamford
Production Runner	Rick Barker
Floor Runner	Daniel Heath
Stunt Co-ordinator	Nick Powell
Script Supervisor	Sheila Wilson
FT2 Continuity Trainee	Victoria Pike
Nurse	Patricia Barr
Camera Operator/ Steadicam	Peter Robertson
Focus Puller	Keith Broome
Clapper Loader	Mark Maidment
Grip	Jim Monks
Camera Trainee	Stuart Chapman
Stills Photographer	Sophie Baker
Sound Recordist	Peter Sutton
Sound Maintenance Engineer	Keith Pamplin
Production Accountant	Martin Cook
Assistant Accountant	Richard Wood
Art Director	Frank Walsh
Assistant Art Director	Paul Kirby
Production Buyer	Roger Hulme
Set Dresser	Claire Grainger
Art Department Junior	Edward Cotton
Assistant Editor	Riaz Meer
Sound Editor	Danny Longhurst
Dubbing Mixer	Mike Narduzzo
Trainee	Marian Vossaugh
Chief Make-up and Hair	Aileen Seaton

Make-up/Hair Artist	Jane Walker
Wardrobe Supervisor	Colin Lavers
Wardrobe Assistant	Anna Houghton
Property Master	Alan Bailey
C/H Stand-by Prop	Dave Fisher
Stand-by Prop	William Edwards
Dressing Prop	Danny Evans
Dressing Prop	Brian Humphrey
Prop Storeman	George Malin
Construction Manager	Alan Chesters
Stand-by Carpenter	Peter Beasley
Stand-by Rigger	Tom Lowen
Stand-by Stagehand	David Gruar
Stand-by Painter	Anthony Caccavale
Gaffer	Joe Ryan
Best Boy	Iwan Williams
Electrician	Terry McGuiness
Electrician	Liam McGill
Stunt Doubles	Joss Gower
	Sy Hollands
Dog Trainer	Rona Brown
Vehicles provided by	H.R.H. Prince Rainier of Monaco
	The Vauxhall Historic Vehicle Collection

PART ONE

<u>EXT. DAY. FRENCH RIVIERA ROCKY COASTLINE. 1927.</u>

DAPHNE is sketching the French coastline. She hears the sound of a car approaching and stops sketching to listen. Looking up behind her at a projecting vantage point on the cliff road above her, she sees MAXIM DE WINTER smoking a cigarette. DAPHNE looks back at her sketch pad and hears his car starting up. When she returns her gaze to the cliff top the figure has disappeared.

<u>INT. NIGHT. MONTE CARLO. 1927. COTE D'AZUR HOTEL. DINING ROOM.</u>

A small string orchestra plays discreetly. Uniformed page boys skip among the tables, delivering messages on little silver trays.

MRS. VAN HOPPER and DAPHNE are having dinner.

> **Mrs. Van Hopper** (V.O.)
> *(laughs)*
> No, not a single well-known personality!
> *(laughs)*
> What's happening to this place! D'you think the management will give me a discount?

She drinks some champagne.

> **Mrs. Van Hopper**
> I mean, what do they think I come here for, you know, to look at page boys?

1

Her gaze settles on one of the BOYS.

Mrs. Van Hopper
That one's cute . . . Once upon a time . . . Are
you shocked? Well sure you are.
(laughs)

*Her eyes suddenly widen with excitement, and she whips up
her lorgnette. MAXIM enters the restaurant and sits at a
table.*

Mrs. Van Hopper
Well now, wait a minute now, here is somebody
– and how! It's Max de Winter, the man who
owns Manderley . . . You have heard of
Manderley, have you?

Daphne
(quietly)
Yes, of course.

*DAPHNE is embarrassed but steals a look. MRS. VAN
HOPPER is busy writing a note to him.*

Mrs. Van Hopper
He's been ill . . . They say he can't get over his
wife's death . . . She drowned . . . in a bay near
Manderley.

MRS. VAN HOPPER gives the note to a passing PAGE BOY.

Mrs. Van Hopper
Here, kiddo – take that to the man over there
with the waiter . . . Quick . . . Quick.

*MAXIM DE WINTER takes the card and nods courteously
at the women.*

Mrs. Van Hopper

Rebecca, his wife was called . . . A beauty! . . . Well weren't we all?

She takes out her mirror to check her appearance.

INT. NIGHT. COTE D'AZUR HOTEL. LOUNGE.

MRS. VAN HOPPER, MAXIM and DAPHNE sit having coffee and liquors.

Mrs. Van Hopper

It's so good of you to join us. You know I did wonder, just that little bit . . . would you remember me?

Maxim

Oh immediately, Mrs. Van Hopper.
(slight pause)
Exactly where . . .

Mrs. Van Hopper
(quickly)
My cousin Billy's birthday. Claridge's. Oh he was so proud to have you for his friend and oh to hear him talk about Manderley – stars in his eyes! A fairyland! I wonder you can bear to leave it. Billy said, you know, that, what do you call it, that, that . . . galleried hall. Oh, he said it was a real gem. I bet Manderley's entertained royalty, huh? Is that so?

Maxim
(slight pause)
Not since Ethelred – the one they call The Unready. My family gave him that name – he was invariably late for dinner.

3

MAXIM looks at DAPHNE – sharing the joke. MRS. VAN HOPPER suddenly gets the joke and laughs.

Mrs. Van Hopper
I like that one! I love a man with humour.
Okay, now that we've broken the ice I hope
we'll see some more of you. Come up to the
suite, have a drink. I often have a few friends
over, you know.

MAXIM lights her cigarette for her.

Maxim
That's very kind of you but I've only just
arrived and I'm not sure how . . .

He turns his attention to DAPHNE to avoid finishing the question.

Maxim
What do you think of Monte Carlo . . . or don't
you think anything of it?

Daphne
I suppose it's . . . artificial in a way, but then
the setting . . .

Mrs. Van Hopper
(cutting in sharply)
But she's spoilt, you know, that's her trouble.
Most girls would give their eyes to see Monte.

Maxim
Wouldn't that rather defeat the purpose?

MRS. VAN HOPPER laughs.

Mrs. Van Hopper
You are the funny one.

INT. NIGHT. COTE D'AZUR HOTEL. DAPHNE'S BEDROOM.

DAPHNE sits in bed sketching a portrait of MAXIM.

INT/EXT. DAY. COTE D'AZUR HOTEL. RESTAURANT TERRACE.

DAPHNE walks to a table and stops abruptly when she hears MAXIM's voice behind her.

Maxim

Good morning.

She turns.

Maxim

Are you alone?

He stands up.

Daphne

Yes.

Maxim

Please, join me.

He gestures for a WAITER to set a place for her and offers her a chair.

Maxim

So how are you this morning?

Daphne

I'm very well thank you.

Maxim

I'm . . . sorry if I was rude last night.

Daphne

You weren't.

5

Maxim

Well, not to you perhaps . . .
(slight pause)
How is your friend this morning?

Daphne

She has a touch of . . . influenza.

Maxim
(mock-gravity)
Poor Mrs. Van Hopper . . . To be treated with
champagne cocktails, perhaps hmmm?

He smiles. The WAITER comes to the table.

Maxim

Poached eggs, toast, English marmalade and
coffee – yes?
(laughs)
Merci.

They smile at each other.

EXT. DAY. COTE D'AZUR HOTEL. GARDENS.

MAXIM and DAPHNE walk in the morning sunshine.

Daphne

She's training me to be what's called a companion. She pays me.

Maxim

I didn't know you could buy companionship.

Daphne

Not the real kind – of course not. I looked up
the word in a dictionary; it said a companion is
a friend of the bosom.

6

Maxim
(laughs)
Don't you have any family?

Daphne
No, my parents are both dead.

Maxim
Oh, we have something in common – we're
both on our own in the world. I do have a sister
and an ancient grandmother but neither of them
make for companionship.

DAPHNE smiles at him.

Daphne
You do have a home though – somewhere of
your own. I bought a picture postcard of
Manderley when I was a child . . . cost half my
pocket money.

He laughs.

Maxim
It's an empty house. Sometimes as lonely as a
full hotel. So what's going to happen to this
friend of the bosom when Mrs. Van Hopper
falls downstairs and breaks her exquisite neck?

Daphne
I suppose there'll be other Mrs. Van Hoppers.

Maxim
Plenty. And at your age such a future holds no
terrors for you, does it?
(slight pause)
Nothing does.
(slight pause)
I'm twice your age.

7

He moves towards her and brushes her hair away from her face. DAPHNE is surprised.

Maxim

Go and put a hat on.

EXT. DAY. ROAD ABOVE MONTE CARLO.

MAXIM and DAPHNE are out for a drive together in the hills.

Maxim

At Manderley you can hear the sea from the terrace . . . the tide washing in and out of the bay . . . Not like it is here . . . cold, grey, like slate but in spring there are masses of flowers ∴ . . daffodils . . . primroses . . . bluebells. But I won't have them picked for the house. Sheer vandalism. Wild flowers are best left where they are. My sister used to complain there were too many scents at Manderley – made her feel drunk, she said . . . I don't care . . . It's the only kind of drunkenness I like . . .

He seems to be getting angry.

Maxim

You crush a petal in your hand – a thousand scents . . . goes straight to your head.

The car begins to get closer and closer to the edge. DAPHNE is terrified and screams.

Daphne

No! No!

MAXIM seems to suddenly snap out of it and stops the car.

Maxim
I'm sorry. That was unforgivable of me. Please don't be frightened.

He takes out his handkerchief and wipes his brow.

Daphne
Shall we go back now?

He nods and reverses the car.

Maxim
There, see, not as dangerous as it looks.

Daphne
Do you know this place? Have you been here before?

Maxim
Yes.
                    (slight pause)
Yes, it doesn't change.

He smiles cheerfully at her.

Maxim
Safely home.

He takes her hand.

Daphne
(faint smile)
Thank you.

Maxim
You're cold.

He reaches in the back of the car.

Maxim

Here, put these on.

They're too big and they both laugh.

INT. NIGHT. COTE D'AZUR HOTEL. MRS. VAN HOPPER'S BEDROOM.

MRS. VAN HOPPER lounges in bed.

Mrs. Van Hopper

So what have you been doing with yourself today?

Daphne

I've been playing tennis with the professional.

DAPHNE tries nonchalantly to tidy up.

Mrs. Van Hopper

Oh, well, whatever he did for your backhand he put some colour in your cheeks. Anyone new arrive?

Daphne

Not that I noticed.

Mrs. Van Hopper

I'd better have the doctor in tomorrow . . . I'm getting my headaches again . . . ooh. Maybe it's just the boredom of the company . . . Where is everybody these days? You know I mean, Monte used to be . . . oh. Come dear.

She gestures for DAPHNE to hand her the tablets.

Mrs. Van Hopper

I mean, where is the old crowd?

She takes her headache tablets.

Mrs. Van Hopper
See anything of Max de Winter?

Daphne
(coolly)
I saw him having breakfast.

Mrs. Van Hopper
Did he have lunch with anybody?

Daphne
He wasn't in the restaurant at lunch time.

Mrs. Van Hopper
There, you see, they say he never mentions her
name . . . I mean he just won't talk about it . . .
and nobody gets near him. I mean you saw him
give <u>me</u> the brush-off. Still, I don't see why I
shouldn't try again . . . when I get back up on
my toes again . . . I'd say Max de Winter's far
too good mannered to turn a lady down twice.

She looks at herself in her hand-mirror.

Mrs. Van Hopper
Even if the lady's not that much of a lady.

EXT. DAY. COTE D'AZUR HOTEL. DRIVE.

*MAXIM waits for DAPHNE outside the Hotel. She comes
down the front steps, sees MAXIM and crosses to the car.*

Maxim
Good morning. Where does madam wish to go
today?

She gives him a bright smile and a shrug and he laughs.

11

<u>EXT. DAY. HILLS ABOVE MONTE CARLO.</u>

Montage sequence with DAPHNE and MAXIM driving in the hills.

DAPHNE taking a photo of MAXIM. Picnicking.

MAXIM and DAPHNE in a rowing boat.

And finally, driving through the French countryside where DAPHNE sees a local VILLAGE GIRL and they wave at each other.

<u>EXT. DAY. HILL TOP VILLAGE. CAFE GARDEN.</u>

They stop to have coffee at a café.

Maxim
What were you going to say?

She shakes her head.

Maxim
I can see you've got something you want to say. What is it?

Daphne
If only there was an invention that could put a memory in a bottle – like scent . . . And it never faded, and it never got stale . . . And then when you wanted it you just opened the bottle – and it would be like living the moment all over again!

Maxim
What moments in your young life would you preserve like that?

Daphne

This one.

He smiles wryly.

Maxim

Is the coffee really that good?

Daphne
(fiercely)

Don't laugh at me! Don't treat me like a silly
child! I know I haven't seen much of the world!
I know I'm not a woman of thirty-six or something dressed in black satin and pearls!

She stops abruptly and starts biting her nails anxiously.

Maxim

Well you wouldn't be here with me if you were.
Stop biting your nails. It's an ugly habit.

She drops her hand.

Daphne

Why do you take me out day after day? If you
think I'm so silly and ugly – why? You're being
kind – is that it? Well don't choose me for your
charity!

*She is close to tears and abruptly stands and walks away a
few paces, keeping her back to him.*

Maxim

Damn my kindness and my charity. I don't have
any.

He goes to her side.

13

Maxim

I ask you out with me because I want you . . .
You're young enough to be my daughter, and I
don't know how to deal with you . . . but I do
know that you've blotted out the past, better
than all the bright lights of a dozen Monte
Carlos.

(pause)

If you don't believe me, say so and I'll move
on. I only stayed because of you.

Daphne

I don't know anything more about you than the
first day we met.

Maxim

Do you want me to go?

She shakes her head.

Maxim

(softly)

Oh to hell with it.

*He tenderly leans down to kiss her hand and then reaches
up to stroke her face.*

Maxim

Promise me something . . . You'll never wear
black satin.

INT. NIGHT. COTE D'AZUR HOTEL. MRS. VAN
HOPPER'S SUITE. SITTING ROOM.

*MRS. VAN HOPPER is giving a cocktail party. People are
dancing the charleston and MRS. VAN HOPPER already
has MAXIM pinned down. DAPHNE moves around the
room, looking after the guests.*

14

Mrs. Van Hopper

No, everyone knows I'm not one to open old wounds and it must be like a knife through the heart every time you think of her, but Max you've just got to let your friends help you, Max you know join us in these little celebrations and have a laugh. You can't brood your life away – it's not fair on the female population, good-looking man like you going to waste!

She is trying very hard to flirt with him.

Mrs. Van Hopper

I can't believe Rebecca would want that, Max.

MAXIM is trying to control his anger.

Maxim

How kind of you to trouble yourself – especially since I scarcely know you, and my wife never did. Now if you'll excuse me, there are things I have to see to.

He manages a tight, polite smile as he makes to move past her. But MRS. VAN HOPPER plants herself in front of him.

Mrs. Van Hopper

No, no, no. Leaving so soon? We've hardly got started. You can stay for a couple more drinks, can't you Max? Hey, everybody! Everybody!

She taps her glass to attract attention.

Mrs. Van Hopper

We are going to drink to Rebecca de Winter!

MAXIM looks furious.

Maxim

Don't speak her name! Not one of you here
knew her! Goodnight!

*He starts to storm out of the room but realises he is still
holding his glass. DAPHNE comes forward to take it from
him.*

Mrs. Van Hopper

Well, pardon me, Mr. Max de Winter. I mean
it's only a little party!

She turns to the others – with a mock-sorrowful shrug.

END OF PART ONE

PART TWO

EXT. DAY. HILLS ABOVE MONTE CARLO.

MAXIM's sports car climbs a winding road. DAPHNE is beside him.

Daphne (V.O.)
You had every right to walk out.

Maxim (V.O.)
I should know better . . . Infantile tantrums at my age.

EXT. DAY. HILL TOP VILLAGE. CAFE GARDEN.

They return to the same café as before.

Daphne
It was just so unexpected . . . You know what a foolish, lonely, unhappy woman she is . . .

Maxim
Huh, to be pitied and put up with hmm? . . . patiently borne?

Daphne
Yes.

Maxim
Perhaps it's simply that I'm not very good at that kind of thing. One of my defects . . . One of my worst, wouldn't you say?

Daphne
You're laughing at me again.

17

Maxim

No, not really . . . It's just that you can be an
awfully solemn little thing at times.

Daphne

A little thing . . . Is that how you see me?

Maxim

Oh don't be hurt. I didn't mean it to. I hope
you'll always be like that to me . . . so natural,
and open.

Daphne

Like a little girl who never grows up?

Maxim

No, I'm not saying that. What I'm saying is that
I hope you'll always be like you.

Daphne

Anyway, what does it matter how you see me?
You could be gone in a few days . . . and you'll
forget all about me.

Maxim

I'm quite sure I won't forget.

Daphne

Your funny, simple-minded little friend?

Maxim

You.

Their eyes meet.

Maxim

Of course I wouldn't forget you.

She smiles.

<u>INT. DAY. COTE D'AZUR HOTEL. MRS. VAN</u>
<u>HOPPER'S SUITE. SITTING ROOM/CORRIDOR.</u>

Mrs. Van Hopper

Do I have to come down and set you straight?

DAPHNE quietly enters the suite and pauses when she sees
that MRS. VAN HOPPER is on the telephone.

Mrs. Van Hopper

Just tell them Mrs. Van Hopper's usual state-
room – okay!

She slams the telephone down and notices DAPHNE.

Mrs. Van Hopper

Oh, there you are – you're never here when I
need you these days . . .

MRS. VAN HOPPER is obviously excited.

Mrs. Van Hopper

Well now we've got work to do. We're packing
up – leaving tomorrow. I'm sick to death of
Europe! How d'you like the sound of New
York?

DAPHNE looks horrified.

Mrs. Van Hopper

What a face! I mean I said New York! I can't
make you out! The chances I'm giving you! I
thought you said you didn't like Monte?

Daphne
(lamely)

I've got used to it.

19

Mrs. Van Hopper

Big of you! Okay, you can just get used to New York!

<u>INT. NIGHT. COTE D'AZUR HOTEL. DAPHNE'S BEDROOM.</u>

DAPHNE lies in bed, sobbing into her pillow. She is remembering her day out with MAXIM.

<u>EXT. DAY. HILLS ABOVE MONTE CARLO.</u>

She is remembering the day with MAXIM, driving through the hills and waving at the little village girl. Only this time it is her waving goodbye to MAXIM.

<u>INT. DAY. COTE D'AZUR HOTEL. DAPHNE'S BEDROOM.</u>

She opens her eyes and stops crying.

<u>INT. DAY. COTE D'AZUR HOTEL. STAIRS & CORRIDOR.</u>

DAPHNE is looking around the hotel for MAXIM.

<u>INT. DAY. COTE D'AZUR HOTEL. MAXIM'S BEDROOM/CORRIDOR WITH MAXIM'S ROOM.</u>

MAXIM is shaving when there is a knock on the door. He wipes his face and walks over to open it.

Daphne

We're going to New York. I've come to say goodbye.

Maxim

No.

INT. DAY. COTE D'AZUR HOTEL. MAXIM'S BEDROOM.

MAXIM finishes shaving and takes out a cigarette.

Maxim

So Mrs. Van Hopper's had enough of Monte Carlo and wants to go home. So do I. She to New York and I to Manderley. Which would you prefer?

He moves across the room to light his cigarette.

Daphne

Don't make a joke about it. It's unfair.

Maxim

I don't make jokes, oh not this early in the morning anyway. Look it's perfectly simple, either you go to New York with Mrs. Van Hopper or you come to Manderley with me.

Daphne

Do you want a secretary or something?

Maxim

No, you little fool, I'm asking you to marry me.

DAPHNE, startled, just looks at him.

Maxim

I'm sorry, I'm being rather a brute to you, aren't I? We ought to be in a conservatory . . . orchids . . . you should be in a white frock . . . there should be a violin playing a waltz . . . well I'm sorry, we'll have to do without all that.

21

Daphne

Stop it, Maxim. I'm not the sort of person . . .
I'm not sure how to explain, but I don't belong
to your sort of world for one thing.

Maxim

What is my world?

Daphne

Well, Manderley. You know what I mean.

Maxim

Nonsense.

He sits down next to her.

Maxim

But you haven't answered my question.

Daphne

Well how can I? I don't know what to say.

Maxim

Do you mind how soon we get married? It can
all be arranged in a few days . . . A licence, a
magistrate, someone.

Daphne

No church? . . . Bells? . . . Choirboys?

Maxim

No. I had that kind of wedding before. Say yes
. . . quickly. We can drive to Venice for the
honeymoon.

Daphne
(delighted)

Venice?

Maxim

Uh huh. All lovers should go to Venice. We can hold hands in a gondola and then take a cruise back to England. I want to show you Manderley.

Daphne

I would be Mrs. de Winter?

Maxim

Mmm, don't you want to be? I thought perhaps you loved me.

Daphne

I do.

Maxim

So it's yes.

Daphne

Yes, Maxim.

He cradles her head and kisses her.

INT. DAY. COTE D'AZUR HOTEL. CORRIDOR.

MAXIM and DAPHNE walk down to breakfast.

Maxim

Listen, don't worry. We'll discuss everything over breakfast.
>   *(to two OLD LADIES)*
Good morning.
>   *(to DAPHNE)*
Food for thought, eh?

Daphne

I have so many thoughts.

23

Maxim
Then we'll have a large breakfast.

Daphne
What about Mrs. Van Hopper?

Maxim
Shall I tell her?

Daphne
(slight pause, then determined)
No, I'll do it. I'll tell her.

Maxim
Well you'd better do it now. I'll be here.

She sets off down the stairs and he calls after her.

Maxim
I'm sure she'll be very happy for us.

They smile at each other.

INT. DAY. COTE D'AZUR HOTEL. MRS. VAN HOPPER'S BEDROOM.

MRS. VAN HOPPER is lounging in bed.

Mrs. Van Hopper
Well, I've got to hand it to you . . . Tennis lessons, huh?

She laughs and lights a cigarette.

Mrs. Van Hopper
Well game, set and match to you kiddo . . .
(laughs)
You been doing anything you shouldn't?

24

Daphne

I'll finish your packing, of course.

Mrs. Van Hopper

Of course. You're going to have to do a lot
more than <u>packing</u> as mistress of Manderley . . .
Think you can handle it? You think you can
handle <u>him</u>? Oh he's a very attactive creature –
sure . . . but . . .
(takes a puff on her cigarette)
But you watch out, little Cinderella – maybe the
prince turns out to be not so charming! You see
his eyes the other night? Tiger, tiger! You ready
for that kind of thing in your bed?!

*DAPHNE clings to her cold composure – speaks as she
makes for the door.*

Daphne

As you said, you don't have much time – I'll
finish the big trunk.

MRS. VAN HOPPER shouts after her.

Mrs. Van Hopper

Good luck kiddo.

<u>INT. DAY. COTE D'AZUR HOTEL. CORRIDOR.</u>

DAPHNE shuts the door behind her and smiles to herself.

<u>EXT. NIGHT. OPEN SEA.</u>

*A cruise liner, bright with lights, moves steadily under the
stars. MAXIM's voice is heard over.*

Maxim (V.O.)

You are the most delightful company, Mrs. de
Winter . . .

25

INT. NIGHT. CRUISE LINER. STATEROOM.

DAPHNE and MAXIM are in bed.

Maxim

But on our last night aboard I think we have to make a public appearance . . . just for appearances' sake.

Daphne
(smiles)
I'll wear my new dress.

Maxim

And I'll be on my best behaviour – very polite to all the old bores.
(little grin)
There's going to have to be quite a bit of that when we get back. Around the county at any rate – at Manderley we please ourselves. I hope you'll love it as much as I do.

They kiss.

INT. NIGHT. CRUISE LINER. BEAUTY PARLOUR.

DAPHNE is getting a make over in the Beauty Parlour.

Daphne

Nothing too bright . . . just something very light, really . . .

Assistant

You can take quite a lot of colour, actually, Madam. We do have all the very latest tones.

Daphne

I'm not used to too much . . . It's an experiment, really.

Assistant
You can trust us, Madam – we know exactly
what's right for you. Now let's see what you
think of this one.

She shows DAPHNE a lipstick.

INT. NIGHT. CRUISE LINER. FIRST CLASS
COCKTAIL BAR.

*MAXIM waits in the lounge for DAPHNE, smoking a
cigarette.*

*He smiles and goes to stand up when he hears DAPHNE's
voice behind him.*

Daphne (V.O.)
Good evening, Mr. de Winter – may I join you?

Maxim
What have you done to yourself? What's all
that muck on your face?!

Daphne
Is it too much? It's a sort of joke really. All the
other women . . . I thought it went with the
dress.

Maxim
I didn't marry a tart!

Daphne
(shocked and hurt)
Maxim! Please.

*He doesn't seem to have heard her. He snatches out his
pocket handkerchief and thrusts it at her.*

Maxim

Wipe it off – now!

He thrusts a handkerchief at her again.

Daphne

No . . . I can't – not here.

Maxim

Are you determined to make a fool of me? I said wipe it off now!

Daphne

Stop it, Maxim . . . I don't understand.

He realises people are looking at them.

Maxim

I think we should go back to the cabin, darling.

He takes back his handkerchief, picks up his cigarettes and they leave.

INT. NIGHT. CRUISE LINER. STATEROOM.

DAPHNE is taking off the make-up, in tears.

Maxim

I'm so sorry! How could I be so stupid? All over a bit of lipstick! All you wanted was to amuse me, and I bite your head off! It's just that you took me by surprise. I promise I'll never do anything so horrible again . . . Say you'll forgive me, please?

DAPHNE smiles through tears of relief.

Daphne

Of course . . . I love you.

She kneels down to kiss him.

EXT. NIGHT. OPEN SEA.

The ocean liner sails on.

EXT. DAY. ROAD. JOURNEY TO MANDERLEY.

DAPHNE and MAXIM in MAXIM's car heading towards Manderley.

EXT. DAY. APPROACHING MANDERLEY.

Maxim
Almost there . . . are you tired?

She gives him a nervous little smile.

Maxim
You can expect a certain amount of curiosity
. . . Everyone'll want to know what you're
like . . .

Daphne
Only natural.

Maxim
But there's no need to be nervous . . . Just be
yourself and they'll love you . . . and here we
are!

They pass through the drive gates. A family stands to watch them.

Maxim
Nice to see you again.

<u>EXT. DAY. MANDERLEY. DRIVE.</u>

Maxim

You don't have to worry about seeing to the
house. Mrs. Danvers is the one for that . . . she
does everything – just leave it to her . . . She's
quite a character in her own way . . . You'll
probably find her a bit stiff at first . . . But take
no notice – it's just her manner . . . Now close
your eyes – I'll tell you when to open them.

DAPHNE does as he says and shuts them.

*They drive up through the Rhododendron drive and MAXIM
stops the car.*

Maxim

Now! Look! There. Do you like it? It's yours.

*They smile at each other. He is enjoying her reaction. They
drive on.*

<u>EXT. DAY. MANDERLEY. FRONT FACADE &
GARDENS.</u>

*The domestic staff and the estate workers are being
assembled on the front steps.*

Frith

Come along, quickly, we haven't got long.
That's right.

<u>EXT. DAY. MANDERLEY. DRIVE & FRONT OF
HOUSE.</u>

*As they drive towards the house, MAXIM sees all the
assembled staff and mutters in irritation.*

30

Maxim

Damn that woman.

Daphne
(nervously)
What's the matter? Who are all these people?

Maxim

Mrs. Danvers has summoned the staff from all
four corners to welcome us . . . She should
know I wouldn't want that kind of thing.
(then briskly)
Ah, Frith . . .

FRITH joins them with a deferential little bow of the head.

Frith

Glad to see you home, sir . . . And Madam too.

*FRITH opens the car door for DAPHNE, whilst MAXIM
gets out his side and comes round.*

Maxim

Give Robert that coat . . .

ROBERT comes forward to take DAPHNE's coat from her.

Maxim

Now you won't have to say a thing. I'll do it.
Well thank you for this welcome . . . it's good
to see you all again . . . I hope you're all in the
best of health, hmmm . . . I must say it's good
to be back among you . . . Thank you . . .

*He smiles and nods at the faces as they pass. DAPHNE
follows him inside.*

INT. DAY. MANDERLEY. GREAT HALL.

Maxim
There . . . all done.

FRITH takes MAXIM's hat and coat. They pass on into the Great Hall.

Mrs. Danvers
Good afternoon, sir . . . Good afternoon,
Madam.

Maxim
Mrs. Danvers . . . Quite a reception . . . Thank
you . . . Meet Mrs. de Winter.

DAPHNE smiles and steps forward to shake hands. MRS. DANVERS takes her hand, looking into her face without a flicker.

Daphne
I'm so pleased to meet you, Mrs. Danvers.

Mrs. Danvers
Thank you, madam . . . I and all the staff at
Manderley are at your disposal.

DAPHNE manages a faint smile. She glances down at their limply clasped hands before MRS. DANVERS releases her.

Maxim
Good . . . Well now you're friends . . . Fine.
Tea, I think, Frith!

INT. DAY. MANDERLEY. GREAT HALL WITH STAIR-CASE & GALLERY

MRS. DANVERS shows DAPHNE upstairs.

Daphne
(quietly)
I hadn't realised the house was quite so big.

Mrs. Danvers
Yes, Manderley is a big house . . . not as big as
some, of course.

*DAPHNE pauses to look around until she realises MRS.
DANVERS is waiting for her.*

Daphne
Sorry to keep you waiting, Mrs. Danvers.

Mrs. Danvers
It's for you to make your own time, Madam. It
is this way.

Daphne
I'm told you've been redecorating.

<u>INT. DAY. MANDERLEY. MAXIM & DAPHNE'S BED-
ROOM.</u>

Daphne
Oh Mrs. Danvers, it's charming.

Mrs. Danvers
I hope I carried out Mr. de Winter's orders.

DAPHNE crosses the room to look out of the window.

Daphne
But you can't see the sea from here.

Mrs. Danvers
No – not from this wing . . . You can't hear it
either – not from this wing, but Mr. de Winter
said you were to have this room. He thought
you'd prefer it.

Daphne

So this wasn't his bedroom before?

Mrs. Danvers

No. When Mrs. de Winter was alive they lived in the west wing, in the most beautiful room in the house . . . looking down to the sea.

Daphne

Mrs. Danvers, I hope we will be friends and come to understand each other . . . You must have patience with me, because you know this sort of life is so new to me, and I do want to make a success of it and make Mr. de Winter happy . . .

Mrs. Danvers

I hope I shall do everything to your satisfaction Madam.

Daphne

Oh, I'm sure you will. I won't want to make any changes.

MRS. DANVERS starts to leave and then pauses.

Mrs. Danvers

Can you tell me when your maid will be arriving, Madam?

DAPHNE looks uncertain.

Mrs. Danvers

Do you wish for one?

Daphne

I don't know . . . I hadn't thought about it.

Mrs. Danvers
It is usual for ladies in your position.

Her stare doesn't waver.

Daphne
Perhaps you would see about it for me. Maybe
some young girl wanting to train.

Mrs. Danvers
It is for you to say, Madam.

*MRS. DANVERS gives a tiny nod, then turns, shutting the
door behind her.*

Daphne
Thank you, Mrs. Danvers.

*DAPHNE looks round the room, looking at all the beautiful
things on the dressing table.*

END OF PART TWO

PART THREE

EXT. DAY. MANDERLEY. HOUSE WITH GROUNDS.

MAXIM is out walking his dog, JASPER.

INT. DAY. MANDERLEY. MAXIM & DAPHNE'S BEDROOM.

DAPHNE stirs, half-awake. She puts out one arm where she expects to find MAXIM, then opens her eyes when she realises he's not there.

EXT. DAY. MANDERLEY. GARDENS.

MAXIM is outside, throwing sticks for JASPER.

INT. DAY. MANDERLEY. MAXIM & DAPHNE'S BEDROOM.

DAPHNE gets out of bed and opens the curtains.

EXT. DAY. MANDERLEY. GARDENS.

MAXIM is now approaching the house.

Maxim
Jasper come! Come!

INT. DAY. MANDERLEY. GALLERY & STAIRS.

DAPHNE is coming down the stairs and stops briefly to admire a painting of a young woman dressed all in white.

INT. DAY. MANDERLEY. DINING ROOM.

DAPHNE is helping herself to breakfast whilst MAXIM reads a letter.

> **Daphne**
> Who's the woman in the white dress?

> **Maxim**
> *(distracted)*
> Who?

> **Daphne**
> In the gallery . . . the woman all in white.

> **Maxim**
> Some great-great-great aunt or other . . .
> Caroline, I think her name was.

> **Daphne**
> She's very beautiful.

> **Maxim**
> *(eating, mumbling)*
> Hmmm . . . I suppose so.

> **Daphne**
> Wonderful eyes . . . young but not young.
> Would you like me to look like that?

> **Maxim**
> No.

> **Daphne**
> Why not?

> **Maxim**
> Because it wouldn't suit you.

37

Daphne

Why wouldn't it?

Maxim

Stop asking silly questions and eat your egg.

She bridles instantly.

Daphne

Maxim . . .

He studies her and softens.

Maxim

Sorry . . . You mustn't mind me . . . Running a
place like Manderley . . . Such a job . . . Lot on
my mind.

He stands abruptly, very brisk.

Maxim

Right, I've got a mass of things to do . . . Think
you can amuse yourself?

He walks to her and gives her a quick kiss.

Maxim

Oh – lunch today . . . sister, brother-in-law,
Crawley, my agent . . . Old Danvers'll see to it.
You don't mind, do you?

*He's gone before she can answer. She starts to eat her
breakfast.*

<u>INT. DAY. MANDERLEY. MAXIM & DAPHNE'S
BEDROOM.</u>

*DAPHNE returns to her bedroom, but stops short when she
sees two MAIDS are making the bed.*

Daphne

Good morning.

Maids

Good morning, Madam.

Awkward, she backs away then goes off downstairs again.

INT. DAY. MANDERLEY. LIBRARY.

DAPHNE wanders around, searching for some matches. FRITH's discreet cough startles her.

Frith

Do you require anything, Madam?

Daphne

I can't find any matches to light the fire . . . It's rather cool in here.

Frith

The fire in the library isn't normally lit until the afternoon, Madam. You'll find a good fire in the morning room.

Daphne

Yes . . . I see.

Frith

If you should wish to have a fire in the library as well I'll give orders, of course, Madam.

Daphne

Oh, no, I wouldn't dream of it. I'll go to the morning room. Thank you, Frith.

Frith

You'll find writing paper in there, Madam. Mrs. de Winter always did her correspondence and

telephoning in the morning room after
breakfast.

Daphne

Yes . . . thank you . . .

*She goes off out of the room, shutting the door behind her
and then pauses uncertainly at the door. FRITH sees her
hesitation.*

Frith

You go through the drawing room, Madam, and
turn to the right.

Daphne

Thank you, Frith.

INT. MANDERLEY. DAY. DRAWING ROOM.

*DAPHNE walks slowly through it, taking in the detail,
hugging herself against the chilly correctness, and hurries
on.*

INT. MANDERLEY. DAY. MORNING ROOM.

*DAPHNE enters the morning room and seeing JASPER in
his basket, leans down to stroke him.*

*She is startled by the phone ringing and nervously picks it
up.*

Daphne
(timidly)

Yes, who is it?

DAPHNE doesn't recognise the voice.

Mrs. Danvers (V.O.)

Mrs. de Winter?

Daphne
(without thinking)
I'm afraid you've made a mistake. Mrs. de
Winter's been dead for over a year.

Mrs. Danvers (V.O.)
It's Mrs. Danvers, Madam, speaking to you on
the house telephone . . . I wondered if you'd
approved the menus for today.

Daphne
Oh . . . I'm sorry . . . yes, I'm sure I do . . .

Mrs. Danvers (V.O.)
They are on the blotter in front of you on the
desk.

Daphne
Yes . . . very suitable . . . very nice indeed.

Mrs. Danvers (V.O.)
Thank you, Madam.

*DAPHNE carefully replaces the phone. Her attention is
caught by a bookmark of REBECCA's on the desk, which
she picks up to have a look at.*

EXT. DAY. MANDERLEY. GARDEN AND WEST WING.

*DAPHNE is studying the west wing and is startled at the
sound of FRANK CRAWLEY's voice.*

Crawley
Good morning!
(DAPHNE reacts)
Sorry. I'm Frank Crawley, Maxim's estate
manager.

Daphne

Yes of course. Maxim's told me about you.
Good morning.

Crawley

Exploring Manderley?

Daphne

There seems to be so much to learn about it.

Crawley

Yes, it's a fascinating old place.

Daphne

Is this side of the house completely shut up?

Crawley

Not exactly . . . it's just that with only the two
of you . . . the west wing isn't needed really.

Daphne

The first Mrs. de Winter used it . . .

CRAWLEY doesn't respond.

Daphne

I imagine she had it all done to her own special
taste.

Crawley

She liked big rooms.

Daphne
(studying the wing again)
With all the shutters closed like that it looks
like . . . forbidden territory.

Crawley

No . . . no, your side of the house has better
light . . . that's what was in Maxim's mind . . .
light and fresh . . . to suit you as we can all see
now.

Daphne

That's very kind of you Mr. Crawley.

INT. DAY. MANDERLEY. GREAT HALL.

*DAPHNE is to start up the stairs when she notices a door
in the corner of the hall which is ajar. On impulse she goes
over to it and enters.*

INT. DAY. MANDERLEY. WEST WING. CORRIDOR &
STAIRS.

*Uneasily, DAPHNE starts up the stairs and pushes open a
door at the top.*

INT. DAY. MANDERLEY. WEST WING. REBECCA'S
BEDROOM.

*DAPHNE takes a look around the room and then, sensing
someone behind her, she spins round and faces MRS.
DANVERS.*

Mrs. Danvers

What do you want here, Madam? Can I help
you?

Daphne
(nervously)

I lost my way.

Mrs. Danvers

Do you want me to show you these rooms? . . .
This is the west wing . . . You can, of course,

see whatever you wish . . . You have only to
ask. I thought you should know your guests
have arrived. Let me show you back to your
side of the house.

Daphne
(rallying a little)
I'm sure I can find it. There's no need.

DAPHNE brushes past her.

INT. DAY. MANDERLEY. WEST WING. CORRIDOR.

DAPHNE rushes towards the stairs, glancing back nervously.

INT. DAY. MANDERLEY. DINING ROOM.

*MAXIM, DAPHNE, BEATRICE, GILES and CRAWLEY sit
at the table having coffee and port.*

Beatrice
We're not a bit alike, you know, my brother and
I. You never know what's going on in that
funny head of his. Me – I lose my temper at the
slightest provocation and bang, it's all over.
Maxim now – he hits the roof once in a blue
moon and how he hits it.
(laughs)
Don't think you'll set him off, though . . .
You'll know how to soothe the savage beast.

Maxim
(exasperated)
Quite intolerable, Beatrice.

Beatrice
Poor Maxim . . . such a ghastly time he had . . .
Perfect wreck six months ago . . . Now you
look much better . . .

She pats his hand affectionately.

Beatrice (cont.)
. . . much better . . . doesn't he, Giles?

Giles
(beaming smile)
You're a different person, old chap – don't you
think so, Crawley?

Crawley
Absolutely.

Maxim
Thank you . . . my God.

Beatrice
Poor Maxim!

She turns her attention back to DAPHNE.

Beatrice
Oh, do you hunt, my dear?

Daphne
Oh I'm afraid not. I learnt to ride as a child –
but very feebly. I don't remember much about
it.

Beatrice
Oh you must take it up again. You can't possibly live in the countryside and not ride – what
would you do with yourself?

Maxim
She sketches and paints . . . rather well.

He gets a grateful smile from DAPHNE.

Beatrice
Very nice, I'm sure, on a wet day when there's nothing better. But there's no exercise in it, is there?

Daphne
I like walking and swimming.

Beatrice
Oh no, the water's far too cold.

Daphne
Oh, I don't mind, as long as the currents aren't too strong. Is it safe to swim in the bay?

A moment of awkward silence as DAPHNE realises what she's said. Then BEATRICE comes to the rescue.

Beatrice
Jasper looks as if he could do with a swim. Been eating too much, old boy? Just like Giles.

Giles
(jovial)
Ah. Give a dog a bad name, eh?

They all laugh, relieved, as GILES puts a chocolate in his mouth.

EXT. DAY. MANDERLEY. HOUSE & DRIVE.

Beatrice

Are you very much in love with him? No, don't answer, I can see what you feel. I'm an interfering bore, aren't I? You mustn't mind me, I'm devoted to Maxim.

GILES toots the car horn impatiently.

Giles
(shouting)
Come on, Bee old girl.

Beatrice
(confidentially)
How're you getting on with the Danvers woman?

Daphne

I've never met anyone quite like her before.

Beatrice

Don't suppose you have ... Thing is – she's insanely jealous of you.

Daphne

Why?

Beatrice

Resents you being here at all – that's the trouble.

DAPHNE's puzzled.

Beatrice

I thought Maxim would have told you – she simply adored Rebecca.

Daphne
I see.

Beatrice
Dare say she'll get over it in time . . .

More toots from GILES's car.

Beatrice
If Maxim doesn't want to talk about it, I
wouldn't try to force it.

Daphne
No, of course.

Beatrice
All part of forgetting Rebecca – if he can. Hell,
that was a tactless damn thing to say! One thing
– you're not a bit like Rebecca!

EXT. DAY. MANDERLEY. WOODS.

*MAXIM leads DAPHNE along a footpath, with JASPER
trotting around them.*

Maxim
A little of my family goes a very long way . . .
And you haven't met Grandma yet.

Daphne
Oh don't be grumpy, Maxim . . . I liked them
. . . Beatrice just says what she thinks.

Maxim
Does she think?

Daphne
She thinks I should do something different with
my hair.

48

Maxim

What's it got to do with her? What the hell's
wrong with your hair?

She takes his arm and smiles at him.

Daphne

So you like my hair?

Maxim

Of course I do. Of course I like your hair.

EXT. DAY. MANDERLEY. FIRST COVE & SEA.

Maxim

It's quite a shock, isn't it? The contrast is so
sudden, after the woods. No-one ever expects it.
Not even me. Jasper! Jasper? . . . Come on, you
stupid dog, where are you?

Daphne

Over there.

She immediately starts for the rocks.

Maxim

No – he can look after himself!

She calls over her shoulder.

Daphne

It's alright, I'll fetch him.

MAXIM stays put – shouts angrily again.

Maxim

He can find his own way back!

EXT. DAY. MANDERLEY. SECOND COVE WITH SEA & COTTAGE.

> **Daphne**
> *(calling)*
> Jasper? Here, Jasper!

DAPHNE spots him running excitedly towards the cottage. She smiles and mutters to herself.

> **Daphne**
> Silly dog.

She starts towards the cottage. BEN, hidden by the rocks, sees her and follows.

> **Daphne** (V.O.)
> Jasper.

INT. DAY. MANDERLEY. SECOND COVE. COTTAGE.

DAPHNE spots JASPER hiding under the sofa bed and crouches down beside it.

> **Daphne**
> *(softly)*
> What's the matter? . . . This isn't a nice place.
> Come on, Jasper, let's go home.

Suddenly JASPER starts to bark at something. DAPHNE turns round and sees a man standing there. She gasps nervously.

> **Ben**
> I know that dog. He comes from the house. He
> ain't your dog.

JASPER growls quietly at him from under the sofa.

50

Daphne

No, he's Mr. de Winter's dog.

She stands up.

Daphne (cont.)

Come on, Jasper . . . good boy.

DAPHNE makes for the door with JASPER following and squeezes past BEN.

EXT. DAY. MANDERLEY. SECOND COVE. COTTAGE.

DAPHNE walks quickly away but BEN follows, calling after her.

Ben

She don't go there now.

Daphne

No, not now.

Ben

Gone . . . in the dark . . . Gone in the sea, ain't she? . . . Won't come back. I never said nothing, did I?

She is disturbed by him and hurries on.

Daphne

No, of course not . . . don't worry.

BEN mutters after her.

Ben

I never said nothing.

A distant rumble of thunder sounds.

EXT. DAY. MANDERLEY. WOODS.

MAXIM strides angrily ahead of DAPHNE. She hurries to keep up with him.

Maxim

It was only Ben. He's perfectly harmless. His father used to be one of the keepers. And that cottage is supposed to be kept locked! Jasper!

Daphne

Wait for me, Maxim.

Maxim

Now if you'd listened to me instead of chasing after that stupid dog we'd be home by now and we wouldn't be getting soaked!

Daphne

Well I was afraid he might get caught by the tide.

He stops to face her.

Maxim

Oh is it likely I would leave the dog if there was any question of danger to him?

Daphne

Well how should I know, in your mood you're capable of anything.

Maxim

Now you're whining because you're tired!

Daphne

I'm not and that's just your excuse.

He glowers at her.

Maxim

Excuse? Excuse for what?

Daphne

For not coming with me over the rocks, I
suppose.

Maxim

And why do you think I didn't want to come
with you?

Daphne

Oh Maxim, how should I know? I'm not a
thought reader.

Maxim

*(spoken at the same time as DAPHNE's speech
below)*

I'm not suggesting that you are but you might
have some . . .

Daphne

I know you didn't want to, that's all. I could see
it in your face.

Maxim

See what in my face?!

She tries to calm him.

Daphne

Please, let's stop this . . . Please, Maxim.

Maxim

All right! I didn't want to go to the other beach!
I never go near the bloody place! I never go to
that damned cottage and you wouldn't either if
you had my memories. You wouldn't talk about

53

it – you wouldn't even think about it! Does that satisfy you?!

Daphne
(softly)
Please, Maxim . . . I don't want you to look like that . . . It hurts too much . . . Please . . .

Maxim
We should have stayed in Italy . . . we should never have come back to Manderley . . . I was a fool to come back.

Daphne
You're all wounded and hurt inside. I can't bear to see you like this . . . I love you so much.

Maxim
Do you? . . .

He pulls her toward him, searching her face.

Maxim
Do you?

Then fiercely he kisses her and folds her in his arms.

EXT. DAY. MANDERLEY – SECOND COVE AND SEA.

BEN, hunched over from the rain, sits looking out to sea.

END OF PART THREE

PART FOUR

INT. DAY. MANDERLEY. MAXIM & DAPHNE'S BEDROOM.

DAPHNE is drying her hair in front of the fire. MAXIM enters and comes to sit behind her.

Maxim
Here.

He takes the towel and starts to rub her wet hair.

Maxim
It was having that crowd for lunch – I should have waited a few weeks . . . Poor old Beatrice, she always gets my goat but I'm quite fond of her really.

Daphne
We will be happy here, won't we?

She turns to look at him.

Maxim
Of course.

They kiss.

Maxim
If you pass Grandma's inspection.

They laugh softly.

EXT. DAY. MANDERLEY. GARDENS.

DAPHNE is cutting some flowers. Satisfied, she gathers them up and heads for the house.

INT. DAY. MANDERLEY. MORNING ROOM.

DAPHNE comes in, carrying a big vase of flowers, trying to decide where to put them. She finally decides on a table near the window, but in setting the heavy vase in position her hand catches a china cupid and it shoots off the table and shatters on the floor.

DAPHNE stares at the remnants, horrified. Hearing voices she guiltily puts the pieces into an envelope and hides them in the desk drawer.

INT. DAY. MANDERLEY. DINING ROOM.

> **Frith** (V.O.)
> Could I speak to you, sir?

MAXIM and DAPHNE are having breakfast.

> **Maxim**
> *(absently)*
> Yes, of course . . . What is it?

> **Frith**
> It's about Robert, sir. There's been a slight unpleasantness between him and Mrs. Danvers, sir. Robert is very upset, he came to me almost in tears, sir.

> **Maxim**
> Oh, Lord.

> **Frith**
> You see, sir, it's one of Robert's duties to change the flowers in the morning room . . .

> **Maxim**
> Yes, Frith, please . . . the problem?

56

Frith

An ornament is missing, sir. Mrs. Danvers has accused Robert of either taking it or breaking it, and hiding the pieces sir.

Maxim

What ornament?

Frith

The china cupid, sir.

Maxim

One of our treasures?

Frith

I believe so, sir.

Maxim

Well, I'll see Mrs. Danvers as soon as I've finished my breakfast.

Frith

Very good, sir.

FRITH leaves the room.

Maxim

Damn – cupid's worth a hell of a lot . . . And I can't stand servants' rows.

DAPHNE looks up at him – nervously.

Daphne

Maxim, I'm sorry . . . I feel such a fool . . .

He looks at her quizzically.

INT. DAY. MANDERLEY. DRAWING ROOM.

FRITH enters, carrying a small silver tray with the pieces of the broken cupid on it.

Maxim

Well, there you are, Mrs. Danvers – one fallen angel. It seems Mrs. de Winter broke it herself and forgot to say anything. Drama over, I hope.

MAXIM stands and takes out a cigarette.

Daphne
(deeply embarrassed)
I'm sorry . . . I didn't think Robert would get into trouble.

Maxim

Well perhaps you'd be good enough Mrs. Danvers to send the pieces up to London. If it's too far gone to be mended, well it can't be helped . . .
(turns to FRITH)
Right, Frith, tell Robert to dry his tears.

Frith

Very good, sir.

He withdraws. MRS. DANVERS doesn't move.

Mrs. Danvers

I will apologise to Robert, of course, but the evidence pointed so strongly to him . . . I would like to ask that if anything similar should happen again, Mrs. de Winter will inform me personally . . . so as to save any unnecessary disturbance at Manderley . . . We try to avoid unpleasantness.

Maxim
Yes, well it looks as though Mrs. de Winter was afraid you'd have her thrown in gaol, doesn't it, Mrs. Danvers? Like some frightened little between-maid.

DAPHNE can't bring herself to look at either of them.

Mrs. Danvers
(prim, cold)
A between-maid at Manderley would never be allowed to touch the valuables in the morning room, sir. We've never had any breakages in the morning room. When Mrs. de Winter was alive she and I always dusted the valuables together. Now there's no-one else I can trust.

Maxim
Yes, well it can't be helped. Thank you, Mrs. Danvers.

MAXIM lights his cigarette.

Mrs. Danvers
Thank you, sir.

MRS. DANVERS picks up the tray and leaves the room.

Maxim
You do such extraordinary things. Why didn't you get hold of the woman as soon as you broke the wretched object and say, 'Here, Mrs. Danvers, get this mended.' She'd understand that.

Daphne
I can't help being shy.

Maxim

I thought you were getting over it.

Daphne

I try. I try every day . . . Every time I go out, or meet someone new . . . I do try – but I've not been brought up to it. It's all very well for you.

Maxim

It's nothing to do with up-bringing, it's just getting on with it. You know damn well that life at Manderley is the only thing that interests anybody down here.

Daphne

I suppose that's why you married me. You knew I was dull and quiet and inexperienced – so there'd never be any gossip about me.

Maxim

What do you mean?

Daphne

I don't know.

Maxim

What do you know about any gossip down here?

Daphne

Nothing . . . Why are you looking at me like that?

Maxim

Who's been talking to you?

Daphne

No-one . . . What have I said?

60

Maxim

You know what you said.

Daphne

It didn't mean anything . . . It just came into my
head . . . really I . . . I don't know why.

Maxim

Well it wasn't a nice thing to say, was it?

Daphne

No, it was stupid . . . horrible . . . I'm sorry.

<u>INT. DAY. MANDERLEY. GREAT HALL.</u>

*MRS. DANVERS has been listening at the door but moves
away when she hears FRITH approaching.*

<u>EXT. DAY. GRANDMOTHER DE WINTER'S HOUSE.</u>

*DAPHNE arrives at GRANDMOTHER's and is helped from
the car by her chauffeur. BEATRICE is already there.*

Beatrice

Hello. Oh you look a little peaky dear.
Anything wrong?

Daphne

Nothing. Really.

Beatrice

Not starting an infant, are you?

Daphne
(awkwardly)

No, I don't think so.

Beatrice

No morning sickness?

Daphne
No.

Beatrice
Doesn't always follow, of course. I didn't turn a hair when Roger was born. Played golf the day before he arrived. Any suspicions – you let me know.

Daphne
Really, there's nothing to tell.

Beatrice
Hope you do produce a son and heir before too long – terribly good for Maxim. Doing anything to prevent it?

Daphne
(embarrassed)
Of course not . . . No.

Beatrice
Oh, don't look shocked. Brides today are up to everything. Damn nuisance if you want to hunt and you land yourself an infant in the first season! Wouldn't matter in your case though – babies needn't interfere with sketching.

BEATRICE laughs.

Beatrice
Come on. Mustn't keep Granny waiting.

They go in.

EXT. DAY. GRANDMOTHER DE WINTER'S HOUSE. VERANDAH & GARDEN.

Grandmother

I want my tea!

Beatrice

It's on its way, Gran. No need to be grouchy.

Grandmother

Why doesn't Nora bring the tea?!

Beatrice

It's coming, Gran.

Nurse

It's watercress sandwiches today.

Grandmother

Oh I like watercress days. Why didn't you tell me it was watercress day?

The NURSE gets up and fusses with the pillows and shawls.

Nurse

Of course I told you. We are forgetful today, aren't we?

BEATRICE mutters to DAPHNE.

Beatrice

I couldn't do that job for a thousand a day.

NORA arrives with the tea.

Grandmother

Why are you so late, Nora?

Nurse

Now we mustn't be naughty.

GRANDMOTHER suddenly notices DAPHNE.

Grandmother
And who are you?! I haven't seen you before –
Bee, who is this child?

Beatrice
Gran, darling, you know perfectly well this is
Maxim's wife. They've just come back to live
at Manderley.

Grandmother
She's not Rebecca! What have you done with
Rebecca? Who said you could live at
Manderley? Tell Maxim to bring Rebecca!

DAPHNE and BEATRICE are both embarrassed.

Beatrice
We shall simply have to go.

Grandmother
She's not Rebecca!

EXT. DAY. GRANDMOTHER DE WINTER'S HOUSE. FRONT DRIVE & GARDEN.

Beatrice
I really don't know what to say . . . it was quite
awful for you.

Daphne
(subdued but calm)
It doesn't matter, Beatrice . . . Please don't
worry about it.

Beatrice
We did tell her – about the wedding . . . and
everything.

Daphne
Please, there's no need to say any more.

Beatrice
I'd forgotten how she always loved seeing
Rebecca . . . always made such a fuss of her, of
course . . . She'd have her rocking with laughter
and of course Rebecca did have this amazing
gift of being so attractive to absolutely everybody . . . It really didn't matter who – men,
women, children, dogs . . . And I suppose, as
far as Maxim's concerned, the poor old lady
can only connect him with Rebecca. Lord, what
a ghastly afternoon! I know you won't thank
me for this!

Daphne
I don't mind, I don't mind.

Beatrice
Giles will be very upset.

Daphne
Well don't tell him, then. What does it matter?
It doesn't matter at all.

DAPHNE turns to get in the car.

<u>EXT. DAY. ROAD TO MANDERLEY.</u>

*DAPHNE is being driven back along the coast road
towards Manderley.*

Maxim (V.O.)
We should never have come back to Manderley.
I was a fool to come back.

*Out of the window, DAPHNE sees FRANK CRAWLEY and
smiles.*

Daphne

I'll walk the rest, Davies.

She leans out of the window.

Daphne

Frank! . . . Walk me back to the house.

Frank

With pleasure.

He helps her out of the car.

Daphne

I've been doing my duty . . . Lunch with the
Bishop and the Bishop's lady.
(*impish smile*)
And tea with grandmother . . . Did I wear the
right hat?

Crawley
(*smiles*)

The perfect hat.

*The car moves on and DAPHNE and CRAWLEY walk
together.*

Daphne

Tell me about Manderley's famous fancy dress
balls?

Crawley

Used to be an annual event . . . quite a big
show. Everyone in the county came. And quite
a crowd from London.

Daphne

On my calls I keep being asked if we're going
to give another.

Crawley

Lot of organisation.

Daphne

I suppose Rebecca did it.

Crawley

Most of it.

Daphne

I'm always being told what a success Rebecca
made of everything . . .

CRAWLEY doesn't look at her.

Daphne

That's what all these invitations to visit are for,
of course . . . for people to look me up and
down . . . Measure me up against Rebecca . . .
Five out of ten, would you say? On average?

Crawley

Please don't think that. I'm sure people find
you as refreshing and charming as I do . . .
Kindness and sincerity and modesty are worth
all the wit and beauty in the world . . . I think.

He is embarrassed. She smiles gently at him.

Daphne

Thank you, Frank . . . I've got you for a friend,
whatever happens, haven't I?

INT. MANDERLEY. DAY. MAXIM & DAPHNE'S BED-
ROOM.

*MRS. DANVERS comes into their bedroom. CLARICE is in
there arranging flowers.*

CLARICE curtseys nervously and scurries out of the room, leaving MRS. DANVERS there.

<u>EXT. DAY. MANDERLEY. DRIVE. GARDEN. HOUSE.</u>

DAPHNE and CRAWLEY are approaching the house.

Daphne
Are they all Rebecca's things at the cottage?

Crawley
Yes.

Daphne
So it was her own little place . . . a special place?

Crawley
(slight pause)
It was just a boat-house, but she had it converted.

Daphne
What did she use it for?

Crawley
Oh . . . moonlight picnics . . . one thing and another.

Daphne
Romantic. Did you ever go to her moonlight picnics?

Crawley
Once or twice.

Daphne
That's where she drowned, isn't it? Tell me how it happened.

Crawley

She was in her boat . . . a little yacht with a cabin . . . Late one night . . . It capsized . . . It can be very squally in the bay . . . She must have drowned trying to swim ashore.

Daphne

She was alone, then?

Crawley

Yes, she often went out alone like that . . . come back in the small hours . . . sleep at the cottage.

Daphne

Did Maxim mind that?

Crawley
(pause)

I don't know.

Daphne

Was she found on the beach?

Crawley

No. About forty miles up channel . . . Two months later . . . Maxim had to go and identify her.

Daphne

I'm sorry . . . You must hate being reminded . . . But I feel I must know . . . to help me understand Maxim . . . for his sake . . . He never tells me anything about Rebecca . . . But I know he thinks about her . . . as if he blames himself somehow.

69

Crawley

No. He is trying to forget. None of us here want to bring back the past.

Daphne

I've never seen any photographs . . . Was Rebecca very beautiful?

Crawley
(simply)

She was the most beautiful creature I ever saw.

INT. DAY. MANDERLEY. MAXIM & DAPHNE'S BEDROOM.

MRS. DANVERS stands watching them from the upstairs window. Her attention is caught by a photograph of MAXIM and DAPHNE on the dressing table.

EXT. NIGHT. MANDERLEY. TERRACE.

MAXIM and DAPHNE are sitting on the terrace. MAXIM is smoking.

Maxim

We'll do it, Frith.

DAPHNE looks at him reproachfully.

Maxim

Thank you.

Frith withdraws.

Maxim

Did I do something very selfish . . . marrying you?

Daphne
(uncertainly)

How do you mean?

Maxim

Perhaps there are too many years between us
... You should have waited, then married a boy
of your own age ... not somebody like me with
half his life behind him.

Daphne

Well age doesn't mean a thing in marriage. Lots
of couples get ...

Maxim
(cutting in)

I don't care about other couples. Just us. It was
my fault. I rushed you into it. I never gave you
a chance to think it over.

Daphne

I didn't want to think it over. There wasn't anyone else. Don't talk as if we made a mistake.
You know I love you ... more than I've ever
loved anything in my life ... You're everything
to me ... everything there is.

But she isn't reaching him.

Daphne

You're disappointed in me, aren't you? You
think I'm not right for Manderley. If that's what
you think I don't want you to pretend anything.
Admit it – and I'll go away. Is that what you
want?

Maxim

Nonsense, it's just your imagination.

Daphne

This all began because I broke the little cupid.

Maxim
(*overlapping*)
Oh damn the cupid! Do you think I care if it's
in ten thousand pieces or not?!

He stands up, throwing his cigarette away.

Daphne

It made you think about Rebecca again . . .
Everything in that room is Rebecca's. That's
how I came to break the cupid . . . No – not on
purpose, of course. But because I was thinking
to myself, 'This is my room now.' So I took
some different flowers in . . . put them where
there never were any flowers . . to change the
room. But, of course, I was clumsy – not a bit
like Rebecca.

She stands up and goes to him.

Daphne

If you really think we can't be happy, please
say so, Maxim.

Maxim

It wouldn't be true. I'm sorry if I . . . seem to
shut you out sometimes . . . it must be difficult
to live with . . . Not much fun . . . I want us to
be happy.

Daphne

Then we are.

He laughs.

Maxim

So that's agreed . . . It's official.

Daphne

Don't laugh at me.

Maxim

No. I'm sorry I have these meetings in London
over the next couple of days.

He goes to help himself to a drink.

Maxim

Leaving you on your own just at the wrong
time.

He pours a drink.

Daphne

I'll be all right . . . Lots to do.

<u>EXT. DAY. MANDERLEY. DRIVE.</u>

ROBERT helps MAXIM to load his car.

Maxim

Thank you Robert.

MAXIM looks up at the window, searching for DAPHNE.

Robert

Better hurry, sir. You don't want to be late. It's
a long drive.

DAPHNE opens the window so that MAXIM can see her.

Maxim

Indeed.

He sees DAPHNE and smiles.

Maxim

Tell Mrs. de Winter I'll telephone her from
London.

Robert

Very good, sir.

*MAXIM climbs into his car and drives away and DAPHNE
closes the window.*

END OF PART FOUR

PART FIVE

EXT. DAY. MANDERLEY. SECOND COVE WITH COTTAGE.

DAPHNE walks along the beach with JASPER. He goes off towards the cottage again.

Daphne
You can't forget her either, can you, Jasper?

JASPER starts barking at the door and BEN comes shambling out.

Daphne
Quiet, Jasper . . . Shush, boy . . . You're not supposed to go in there, Ben. Mr. de Winter doesn't like it.

Ben
(mumbling)
Done nothing wrong.

Daphne
What have you taken, Ben? Show me.

He obeys like a small child – showing her a length of fishing line.

Daphne
Well, you can have it. But you mustn't do it again . . .

Ben
You've got angel's eyes . . . not like the other one . . .

Daphne

It isn't honest, taking other people's things. You could get into trouble.

Ben

You won't put me in the asylum? Done nothing wrong. I never told no-one.

Daphne

What do you mean, Ben?

DAPHNE stares at him – puzzled, unnerved.

Ben

She eyes like a snake . . . come at night . . . I looked in on her once – she turned on me. She said, 'You ain't seen me here and you won't again.' She said, 'Let me see you looking on me again, I'll have you put in the asylum.' She said, 'They're cruel to people in the asylum.' She's gone now, ain't she? She won't come back?

Daphne

I don't know who you mean, Ben. But no-one's going to put you in the asylum. You mustn't worry about that. I think you should go home now, Ben.

Ben

Angel's eyes.

He reaches for her face but she backs away.

EXT. DAY. MANDERLEY. WOODS.

DAPHNE hurries back, obviously disturbed by BEN.

76

Daphne
He's just a poor, sad thing, Jasper . . . Can't
know what he's saying . . . Stupid to even think
about it . . . Poor, sad, sad thing . . .

She starts running away.

EXT. DAY. MANDERLEY. LAWN & WOODS.

DAPHNE lies on the grass with JASPER.

Daphne
I'm a silly . . . timid . . . hysterical . . . school-
girl Jasper . . . Let's go home.

As she stands up, she looks up at the house.

EXT/INT. DAY. MANDERLEY. WEST WING OF HOUSE. GARDEN.

She can see a man in the window with MRS. DANVERS.

Daphne
I'm not in the mood for visitors, are you? We'll
keep out of their way.

She picks up her sketching pad and moves off.

INT. DAY. MANDERLEY. MORNING ROOM.

*DAPHNE comes into the room and immediately spots the
cigarettes and lighter on the table.*

Mrs. Danvers (V.O.)
She's come back early for some reason. She's
probably gone to the library. If you hurry
there's no reason why she should see you.

*On hearing the voices, DAPHNE tries to back out of the
room but realises it is too late. JASPER rushes to greet
FAVELL.*

Favell (V.O.)

I left my cigarette case – I'll just go and fetch
it. Hullo, you little tyke . . . Not forgotten me,
then . . .

*FAVELL bends down to pat JASPER and then enters the
morning room. He sees DAPHNE.*

Favell

Oh I do beg your pardon. Too bad of me to butt
in on your privacy like this.

Daphne

It's quite all right.

Favell

The fact is, I just popped in to see old Danny –
she's an old friend of mine.

He spots his cigarette case and goes and picks it up.

Favell

That's the fellow I'm after.

He opens the case and offers her a cigarette.

Daphne

I don't smoke, thank you.

He takes one himself.

Favell

How's old Max?

Daphne

He's very well, thank you . . . He's in London
today.

Favell

And left the bride all alone? Very neglectful.
Isn't he afraid someone'll come and carry you
off? I would be.

*He turns to look at MRS. DANVERS who has entered the
room.*

Favell

Well aren't you going to introduce me, Danny?
It's the usual thing to do, isn't it – pay one's
respects to the bride?

Mrs. Danvers

This is Mr. Favell, Madam. Mrs. de Winter's
cousin.

Daphne

How do you do, Mr. Favell. Can I offer you a
sherry?

FAVELL laughs.

Favell

Now isn't that a charming invitation?

He looks at MRS. DANVERS.

Favell

What about it, Danny? Shall I stay for a sherry?
No, perhaps not. But thanks all the same . . .
Mrs. de Winter . . .
                    (pause)
Sherry and a little chat might have been a lot of
fun.

He draws on his cigarette.

Favell

Dear old Manderley.

He blows smoke up at the ceiling, follows it with his eyes.

Favell

But I'd better be going.

Daphne

I'll see you out, Mr. Favell.

Favell

Right . . . Oh come and see my car – she's a beaut. Danny?

Mrs. Danvers

No, thank you. Goodbye, Mr. Jack.

Favell

Bye, Danny . . .

(grins)

Happy days, eh?

Expressionless, MRS. DANVERS watches them leave.

EXT. DAY. MANDERLEY. DRIVE.

Favell

Look, you'd be doing me a big favour if you didn't mention this little visit of mine to Max.
(regretful smile)
He doesn't exactly approve of me. I've never known why . . . and it might get poor old Danny into trouble.

Daphne

All right.

Favell

Thanks . . . There, isn't she lovely? Goes twice
as fast as Max's old bucket.

He jumps in the car.

Favell

You know, I do call it a damn shame, old Max
jaunting up to London and leaving you all alone
like this.

Daphne

I don't mind being alone.

Favell

Yes but it's all wrong. It's against nature. I
mean, how long have you been married, three
months?

Daphne

About that.

Favell

I wish I had a young bride of three months
waiting for me at home.

He starts the car up.

Favell

I'm a poor, lonesome bachelor. Fare you well.

The car shoots forward.

INT. DAY. MANDERLEY. WEST WING. CORRIDOR.

DAPHNE heads for Rebecca's room again.

INT. DAY. MANDERLEY. WEST WING. REBECCA'S BEDROOM.

She enters and shuts the door behind her.

Daphne

Rebecca.

She crosses the room towards the dressing table and picks up some scent to sniff it. Then she goes to the bed and pulls REBECCA's nightdress out of its bag and holds it against her, smelling it.

Daphne

Rebecca.

Suddenly she drops the nightdress and rushes to the window, opening it to get some fresh air.

Mrs. Danvers (V.O.)

Is anything the matter, Madam?

DAPHNE turns, startled.

Mrs. Danvers

Are you unwell?

DAPHNE falters.

Daphne

No . . . I'm quite all right . . . I saw from the garden the shutters were open.

Mrs. Danvers

You wanted to see her room, didn't you? Of course you did. You've been wanting to see it for a long time, haven't you? Now you're here, let me show you everything.

She puts her arm around DAPHNE's shoulders and leads her towards the bed.

Mrs. Danvers
Isn't it a beautiful bed? You've been touching her nightdress . . .

MRS. DANVERS holds it up.

Mrs. Danvers
The scent is still fresh, isn't it? You can almost imagine she'd only just taken it off. I keep everything as it was on the night she never came back . . . Ready for her . . . just as it always was.

MRS. DANVERS picks up REBECCA's dressing-gown and holds it against DAPHNE.

Mrs. Danvers
See how tall she was . . . It touches the ground on you. She had a lovely figure . . . tall and slim . . . And yet lying there in bed she looked just a slip of a girl, with her mass of dark hair round her face . . . I used to brush her hair every evening . . . twenty minutes at a time . . . It came down below her waist when she was first married. I used to do everything for her. Let me show you her clothes . . .

She takes DAPHNE over to the wardrobe.

Mrs. Danvers
She could wear any style . . . stand any colour . . . The clothes she was wearing the night she was drowned were torn from her body in the water. There was nothing on her at all when she

83

was found all those weeks later. The rocks had battered her to bits. Her beautiful face. Mr. de Winter identified her. He insisted. He was very ill, but no-one could stop him.

Daphne

Please . . .

MRS. DANVERS closes the wardrobe.

Mrs. Danvers

Now you know why Mr. de Winter doesn't come here any more. Listen to the sea . . . Never since the night she drowned . . . He'd sit up night after night in the library . . . in the morning cigarette ash around the floor. And then all day, he'd pace up and down, up and down. No, he never comes here . . .

Her eyes bore into DAPHNE's.

Mrs. Danvers

No-one ever comes here but me. You wouldn't think she was dead, would you? . . . I feel her everywhere . . . So do you, don't you?

DAPHNE wants to drag herself away – but can't.

Mrs. Danvers

I hear her footsteps behind me . . . Or the sound of her dress sweeping the stairs as she comes down to dinner . . .
> (pause)

Do you think the dead come back to watch the living? . . . Is she watching us now?

DAPHNE struggles to speak.

Daphne

No . . . I don't know . . . No.

Mrs. Danvers

Does she watch you and Mr. de Winter together?

DAPHNE stares back – appalled, sick with revulsion, and then she runs from the room.

INT. DAY. MANDERLEY. UPPER CORRIDOR.

In the sinister half-light DAPHNE is running – a desperate, stumbling flight down the stairs – away from MRS. DANVERS.

INT. DAY. MANDERLEY. MAXIM & DAPHNE'S BEDROOM.

She bursts into the safety of her own room and falls on the bed sobbing.

Daphne

Maxim . . . Maxim . . . Maxim.

As she closes her eyes we see:

DAPHNE'S FANTASY.

She is imagining she is making love with MAXIM.

Ben (V.O.)

She has eyes like a snake.

Crawley (V.O.)

She was the most beautiful creature I ever saw.

Mrs. Danvers (V.O.)

Does she watch you and Mr. de Winter together?

INT. DAY. MANDERLEY. MAXIM & DAPHNE'S BEDROOM.

She opens her eyes and scrambles off the bed – dashes to the door to lock it and then over to close the curtains. Then she gets back on the bed – burrowing into it.

INT. NIGHT. MANDERLEY. MAXIM & DAPHNE'S BEDROOM.

The sound of a car arriving. Headlights sweep across the room. DAPHNE slowly wakes and sits up.

EXT. NIGHT. MANDERLEY. HOUSE. GARDEN. DRIVE.

MAXIM's car arrives and pulls up. MAXIM gets out and enters the house.

INT. NIGHT. MANDERLEY. HALL & STAIRCASE.

DAPHNE can hear MAXIM's raised voice and comes out on the staircase to listen.

Maxim (V.O.)
Nonsense. You know my views. I've made them clear to you.

Mrs. Danvers (V.O.)
Might I ask, sir, how you came to hear of this?

INT. NIGHT. MANDERLEY. LIBRARY.

Maxim
Never mind who told me. It's of no importance! I happen to know he was here this afternoon – when you knew I would not be!

Faye Dunaway as Mrs Van Hopper.

Diana Rigg as the sinister Mrs Danvers.

Preparations get under way for the grand fancy dress ball at Manderley

The second Mrs de Winter descends the stairs dressed as Caroline de Winter.

The guests enjoy the fireworks in the grounds of Manderley.

Maxim comforts his frightened wife after he has refused to give in to
Favell's blackmail.

Dr Baker (Timothy West) breaks the news to Jack Favell (Jonathan Cake),
Col Julyan (Anthony Peto) the second Mrs de Winter and Maxim, that Rebecca had been suffering from cancer

The firemen prepare to put out the blaze that is engulfing Manderley.

INT. NIGHT. MANDERLEY. HALL & STAIRCASE.

Maxim (V.O.)
I won't have Jack Favell inside the gates. You
can write and tell him from me to keep away!

INT. NIGHT. MANDERLEY. LIBRARY.

Maxim
If you want to see him you can do so outside
Manderley. Do you understand? I won't warn
you about this again!

MRS. DANVERS says nothing and leaves the room.

INT. NIGHT. MANDERLEY. HALL & STAIRCASE.

DAPHNE watches MRS. DANVERS from up above.

INT. NIGHT. MANDERLEY. LIBRARY.

MAXIM finishes his drink.

INT. NIGHT. MANDERLEY. MAXIM & DAPHNE'S BEDROOM.

*DAPHNE hears MAXIM approaching and shuts her eyes,
pretending to be asleep.*

*He moves to the bed and stands over her, looking at her
peaceful face. He bends down and gently kisses her fore-
head. Her eyes open and she looks up at him. She reaches
for him, they kiss, gently and then again more passionately.*

EXT. DAY. MANDERLEY. GARDEN.

MAXIM, DAPHNE, CRAWLEY, BEATRICE and GILES are having tea on the lawn.

Beatrice
(effusive)

Oh Maxim, do say yes – don't be an old stick
in the mud. It's a splendid idea. It's just what
you need, my dear, to set you up properly as the
new mistress of Manderley. The fancy dress
ball always was <u>the</u> show of the year. Top dog!

Giles

Grand sight – Manderley all lit up. I love fireworks!

Daphne

It does sound a little daunting.

Beatrice

Oh you'll carry it off.

Crawley

You wouldn't have to do anything alarming . . .
Just receive the guests and dance the night
away with all the Charlie Chaplins and
Napoleons.

Maxim
(mock distaste)

Yes, my God – the whole county making fools
of themselves.

Beatrice

He always groans, and he always enjoys it in
the end.

Maxim
(shrugs it off – but amiably)

Do I?

Beatrice

That's a yes.

Giles
(smiles)

Yippee, old boy.

Daphne

What will you wear, Maxim?

Maxim

Oh, I never dress up – it's the one perk I insist on. But what about you? Little Bo Peep? Alice in Wonderland?

Daphne
(spirited)

No, nothing like that.

Crawley

What then?

Daphne
(little smile)

Wait and see – you might get the surprise of your life, Maxim.

Maxim
(mock alarm)

Oh, Lord.

Smiles all round. Then DAPHNE is serious.

Daphne

I'd like to help organise.

Maxim
(quickly)
No, no, no, no, no. You leave all that to Frank
and old Danvers – they know the form.

Giles
Quite right – never volunteer, my dear. You just
have fun!

DAPHNE smiles back warmly at him.

INT. DAY. MANDERLEY. MAXIM & DAPHNE'S BED-ROOM.

*DAPHNE sits at a table sketching ideas for her costume.
CLARICE is busily laying out evening clothes on the bed.*

DAPHNE puts down her pencil and frowns.

Daphne
Come and look, Clarice.

CLARICE comes over and looks over her shoulder.

Daphne
Which do you like best?

Clarice
Oh, Madam, they look beautiful.

Daphne
Hmm . . . I'm not sure.

Clarice
Oh Madam, it's so exciting. Mr. Frith says it
will be just like old times. You should hear
Mother talking about it, she's thrilled to bits.

Daphne
It has to be something really special.

Clarice
(excited)
Oh Madam, it'll be wonderful.

INT. DAY. MANDERLEY. LIBRARY.

DAPHNE sits on the floor surrounded by bulky old volumes, opened at portraits. She turns the pages, lost in concentration.

She is abruptly startled by MRS. DANVERS' voice – soft but close at hand. She looks up.

Mrs. Danvers
Deciding what to wear at the ball, Madam?

Daphne
Nothing seems quite suitable, Mrs. Danvers.

Mrs. Danvers
I wonder you don't copy one of Manderley's own pictures . . . in the gallery.

Daphne
I hadn't thought of that.

Mrs. Danvers
It's not for me to suggest, but . . . if you'll forgive me, Madam, I remember how much you admired the portrait of the young lady all in white.

Daphne
(simply)
Yes, I do . . .
(smiles)
Thank you, Mrs. Danvers.

Daphne
Oh I should need a wig, of course, as well as
the costume.

Mrs. Danvers
I know of some excellent shops in London that
take care of all that sort of thing.

Daphne
And it would have to be kept a secret – to surprise Mr. de Winter.

Mrs. Danvers
(thin smile)
I think I know how to keep a secret, Madam.

INT. NIGHT. MANDERLEY. GALLERY & STAIRS.

*DAPHNE is staring at the portrait of the woman in white.
Satisfied, she turns and goes off downstairs.*

Watching from underneath the staircase is MRS. DANVERS.

INT. NIGHT. MANDERLEY. DINING ROOM.

DAPHNE stares, distractedly, into space. MAXIM notices.

Maxim
What the devil are you thinking about?

Daphne
Hmm oh . . . nothing.

Maxim
(amused, but puzzled)
You look like a little criminal . . . What is it?

Daphne
(little laugh)
Nothing . . . Really.

Maxim

What goes on in the tortuous minds of women
would baffle anyone.

She smiles at him.

Maxim

I don't like to think of you as a scheming kind
of woman.

DAPHNE smiles mischievously back at him.

EXT. DAY. MANDERLEY. GARDEN & TERRACE.

*A bustle of activity in the garden. ESTATE STAFF hurry
along with wheelbarrows full of flowers; CRAWLEY is
supervising.*

INT. DAY. MANDERLEY. MAXIM & DAPHNE'S
BEDROOM.

*CLARICE comes into their bedroom carrying some parcels.
She is clearly excited.*

EXT. DAY. MANDERLEY. GARDEN & TERRACE.

*The preparations continue. Lights being put up. CRAWLEY
still in the midst of it all.*

INT. DAY. MANDERLEY. MAXIM & DAPHNE'S BED-
ROOM.

*DAPHNE comes into the room. CLARICE shows her all the
parcels that have arrived. They are both excited.*

INT. DAY. MANDERLEY. DRAWING ROOM.

*FRITH is supervising the arrangements in the drawing
room.*

INT. DAY. MANDERLEY. MAXIM & DAPHNE'S BEDROOM.

DAPHNE starts unwrapping the parcels.

INT. DAY. MANDERLEY. DRAWING ROOM.

FRITH inspects the crystal.

EXT. DAY. MANDERLEY. DRIVE.

The MUSICIANS have arrived.

INT. NIGHT. MANDERLEY. GREAT HALL WITH STAIRS & GALLERY.

Up in the gallery the small dance ORCHESTRA are warming up. There is a great bustle of last-minute preparations: MRS. DANVERS and FRITH calmly supervising servants as they pass to and fro with great gleaming trays of food and glasses, disappearing into other rooms.

INT. NIGHT. MANDERLEY. MAXIM & DAPHNE'S BEDROOM.

CLARICE is helping DAPHNE get dressed.

Clarice
It's perfect, Madam . . . Fit for a queen, Madam
. . . It's so handsome.

DAPHNE admires herself, twisting and turning to watch the dress.

Daphne
Oh yes it is, it is, it is . . . Clarice, oh it is . . .
Now the wig, Clarice.

There is a knock at the door.

<u>INT. NIGHT. MANDERLEY. UPPER CORRIDOR & DOOR TO BEDROOM.</u>

Beatrice (V.O.)
Are you ready?

<u>INT. NIGHT. MANDERLEY. MAXIM & DAPHNE'S BEDROOM.</u>

Daphne
Beatrice? You can't come in!

<u>INT. NIGHT. MANDERLEY. UPPER CORRIDOR & DOOR TO BEDROOM.</u>

Beatrice
Oh I'm dying to see you! Do come on before
the mob arrive!

<u>INT. NIGHT. MANDERLEY. MAXIM & DAPHNE'S BEDROOM.</u>

Daphne
Just another minute. Wait for me downstairs!

<u>INT. NIGHT. MANDERLEY. UPPER CORRIDOR & DOOR TO BEDROOM.</u>

Beatrice
(big grin)
This had better be good!

She turns away with a noisy laugh.

<u>INT. NIGHT. MANDERLEY. MAXIM & DAPHNE'S BEDROOM.</u>

Daphne
Now the hat.

95

CLARICE carefully places the hat on her head.

Clarice
Oh, Madam, What will Mr. de Winter say?

Daphne
(proud & pleased)
Oh yes. What will he say?

She takes the folds of the skirt in one hand and studies herself in the mirror.

<u>INT. NIGHT. MANDERLEY. GREAT HALL WITH GALLERY & STAIRS.</u>

Everyone is grouped at the bottom of the stairs, with a drink, waiting for DAPHNE.

Maxim
I can't imagine what's going on . . . She's been up there for hours.

Giles
(benign smile)
Big occasion for her, old boy.

CLARICE enters the gallery and directs the drummer to start the drum roll as DAPHNE comes down the stairs.

Everyone looks up in astonishment when they hear the drum roll.

Drummer
Miss Caroline de Winter!

Beatrice
(gasps)
Oh!

MAXIM strides furiously up the stairs towards her.

96

Maxim

What the hell do you think you're doing?

Daphne

It's the picture . . . the white dress . . .

Maxim

Go and change now. Now! Before anybody comes!

Daphne

Change? . . .

Maxim

Yes, change. It doesn't matter what you put on. Anything will do.

She can't move.

Maxim

Well what are you standing there for? Didn't you hear what I said?

She turns blindly and stumbles up the stairs, starting to weep as she runs.

<u>INT. NIGHT. MANDERLEY. CORRIDOR TO MAXIM & DAPHNE'S BEDROOM.</u>

DAPHNE pauses in the corridor, too upset to move, until she notices MRS. DANVERS standing watching her. She tries to pull herself together and walks past MRS. DANVERS.

<u>INT. NIGHT. MANDERLEY. MAXIM & DAPHNE'S BEDROOM.</u>

DAPHNE's disgarded outfit lies on the bedroom floor.

Beatrice

Of course I knew at once it was just a terrible
mistake. You couldn't possibly have known –
why should you?

*BEATRICE sits on the bed, holding DAPHNE's hand, trying
to comfort her.*

Daphne
(quietly)

Know what?

Beatrice

About the dress . . . the picture you copied. It's
exactly what Rebecca did for the last fancy
dress ball. Identical . . . There you stood at the
top of the stairs, and for one ghastly moment I
really thought . . . Well, it's over now . . . You
poor dear, how were you to know?

Daphne
(flat, quiet)

I ought to have known.

Beatrice

Nonsense – it wasn't the sort of thing that could
possibly occur to any of us. But it was such a
shock, you see, and Maxim . . .

She stops, losing her nerve a little.

Daphne
(same tone)

Yes, Maxim?

Beatrice
(plunging on)
Well, Maxim thinks, you see, that it was
deliberate on your part – because you did tell
him you'd surprise him, didn't you? And for
him it was the most frightful shock – you can
imagine . . .

Daphne
(same tone)
Yes . . . I should have known . . . I should have
seen.

Beatrice
No, no! Look, don't worry – you'll be able to
explain the whole thing to him quietly.
Everything'll be hunky-dory. We can tell everyone that the shop sent the wrong costume and
that you're coming down in ordinary evening
dress instead, hmmm?

She gets up and goes toward the wardrobe.

Beatrice
Now let's find something nice.

*DAPHNE doesn't move. A new bitterness hardens her tired
voice.*

Daphne
Why not? Make anything up. What does it
matter?

Beatrice
That's the way . . . For Maxim's sake.

INT. NIGHT. MANDERLEY. GREAT HALL WITH STAIRS & GALLERY.

The fancy dress ball in full swing. Everyone is having a great time except for MAXIM and DAPHNE who stand awkwardly together at the foot of the stairs.

A guest dressed as ADMIRAL NELSON comes up to them.

Admiral Nelson
Heard about the mix-up over the outfit . . . Sue
the shop! I would! Show 'em what's what!
England and Manderley expect – damn-it-all!

He gives a drunken shout of laughter and he and LADY HAMILTON move away. MAXIM and DAPHNE retain their fixed composure.

He is followed by a guest dressed as a TUDOR LADY who comes up to DAPHNE.

Tudor Lady
I think you've done wonders, darling . . .
considering. And it's a sweet little frock really.

She skips away. But then a drunken, paunchy NAPOLEON rams his face close into DAPHNE's.

Napoleon
Tonight, Josephine? Sorry, de Winter –
Emperor's prerogative!

He drags DAPHNE on to the dance floor.

A little later. DAPHNE is still dancing with NAPOLEON when they collide with BEATRICE and a guest dressed as BONNIE PRINCE CHARLIE.

Beatrice

Whoops, my dear! This bonny prince is much
better on a horse . . . Meet Colonel Julyan . . .

Colonel Julyan

Charmed, Mrs. de Winter.

He bows.

Beatrice

Doesn't look the pillar of rectitude one would
expect from a district magistrate, does he?
Come on Charlie.

*MAXIM still stands expressionless and motionless at the
foot of the stairs.*

EXT. NIGHT. MANDERLEY. HOUSE WITH TERRACE
& GARDENS.

*The fireworks display has begun. There are exclamations of
delight from the group.*

Giles
(bellowing)
Capital! Well done, Manderley!

They all clap except for DAPHNE and MAXIM.

INT. NIGHT. MANDERLEY. GREAT HALL.

*An instant change of tone as the assembled company sing
'God Save the King'.*

INT. NIGHT. MANDERLEY. MAXIM & DAPHNE'S
BEDROOM.

MAXIM sits on the bed facing DAPHNE.

Daphne

Let's stop pretending. You don't love me. You
love Rebecca. You've never forgotten about her.
You think about her night and day . . . Rebecca,
Rebecca, Rebecca . . .

He stands up.

Maxim

No, you're wrong.

Daphne

What does it matter that I love you? What kind
of love is that to you – like a child or a pet
dog?

Maxim

No!

Daphne

You want something else I can't give you –
what you had with her. You belong to Rebecca.

Maxim

I have to tell you . . .

He starts towards her – but she backs away in rejection.

Daphne

No! Don't touch me! I'm not Rebecca! But
she's here . . . in this room . . . I can smell the
scent she wears.

Again he tries to go to her.

Maxim

Please!

Daphne

No! . . . No!

Anguished, MAXIM turns and blunders out of the room.

INT. NIGHT. MANDERLEY. HALL & STAIRCASE.

MRS. DANVERS watches MAXIM as he goes downstairs and leaves the house.

INT. NIGHT. MANDERLEY. MAXIM & DAPHNE'S BEDROOM.

DAPHNE, visibly shaken, opens the window and draws breaths of air.

Daphne

I am not Rebecca.

EXT. NIGHT. MANDERLEY. WOODS.

MAXIM walks down the path towards the sea.

EXT. NIGHT. COVE AND SEA.

MAXIM sits down to have a cigarette, brooding, looking out into the bay.

END OF PART FIVE

PART SIX

EXT/INT. MANDERLEY. DAY. HOUSE. TERRACE. GARDEN.

The morning after. It is misty. GARDENERS and OTHER STAFF are clearing up.

INT. DAY. MANDERLEY. MAXIM & DAPHNE'S BEDROOM.

DAPHNE is huddled in an eiderdown looking out of the window. She moves to sit in a chair.

EXT. DAY. MANDERLEY.

The foghorns are sounding their warning.

INT. DAY. MANDERLEY. DINING ROOM.

DAPHNE enters and takes in the empty room.

Frith
Good morning, Madam. We cleared away. But if you would like breakfast . . .

Daphne
No, that's quite all right, Frith – it is late. Did Mr. de Winter have breakfast?

Frith
Ah no, Madam.

Daphne
Is he in the library?

Frith

No, Madam. I haven't seen Mr. de Winter this morning.

She goes out again.

EXT. DAY. MANDERLEY. GARDEN.

Three or four GARDENERS are clearing up with rakes and wheelbarrows. DAPHNE walks towards them. They touch their caps as she approaches.

Daphne

Good morning. I'm afraid last night we made a lot of work for you.

Oldest Gardener

As long as everyone enjoys themselves, that's what really matters, isn't it Madam?

Daphne

Yes, of course. Have you seen Mr. de Winter yet?

Oldest Gardener

No, Madam, not yet, not this morning.

Daphne

Thank you.

EXT. DAY. MANDERLEY. GARDEN & WOODS.

DAPHNE continues to search for MAXIM. The foghorns are still sounding. She spots CRAWLEY talking to some ESTATE WORKERS and runs towards him.

Crawley

Carry on then. Is anything the matter?

Daphne

I <u>must</u> find Maxim. Have you seen him?

Crawley

Well he hasn't been in the estate office. He's probably taken himself off for a long walk . . . morning after, you know? It must have been very distressing for you.

Daphne

He didn't come to bed last night, Frank. I said things to him, I didn't let him answer.

Crawley

(reassuring)

You're still tired, get some more rest until he comes back.

(gently)

You mustn't blame yourself. You weren't to know about the dress. Look, I've got to get going. Don't worry too much about Maxim, he'll turn up when he's ready. It's his way.

More foghorns. DAPHNE is really worried.

INT. DAY. MANDERLEY. WEST WING. CORRIDOR.

Angry, DAPHNE strides with grim purpose along the corridor to REBECCA's rooms.

INT. DAY. MANDERLEY. REBECCA'S BEDROOM.

DAPHNE enters, closing the door firmly behind her. MRS. DANVERS is there, lovingly dusting Rebecca's things.

Daphne

You've done what you wanted, haven't you?
Are you happy now, Mrs. Danvers? You made
me wear that dress last night. You did it just to
hurt Mr. de Winter – to make him suffer. Hasn't
he suffered enough. Do you think his pain can
bring Rebecca back again?

MRS. DANVERS turns to face her, her voice bitter.

Mrs. Danvers

What do I care about his suffering? He's never
cared about mine! How do you think I've felt –
watching you take her place, walk in her footsteps, touch the things that were hers? What do
you think that's meant to me all these months –
hearing the servants calling you Mrs. de
Winter?!

Mrs. Danvers

And all the while <u>my</u> Mrs. de Winter lying dead
and forgotten in the church crypt! He deserves
to suffer, marrying a chit of a girl like you not
ten months after!

DAPHNE is too astonished by the outburst to answer.

Mrs Danvers

Well, he's paying for it, isn't he? He's made his
own hell and he's no-one but himself to thank
for it!

Daphne

It isn't true. We were happy together.

DAPHNE moves closer to Mrs. Danvers.

Mrs. Danvers
On your honeymoon? He's a man, isn't he? Of course he enjoyed himself.

DAPHNE steps right up to her, coldly angry, and grips her arm.

Daphne
How dare you speak to me like that.

For a moment MRS. DANVERS is taken by surprise.

Mrs. Danvers
A bit of spirit, after all.

She walks towards the window.

Mrs. Danvers
Spirit . . . No-one could match my lady for spirit . . . I looked after her ever since she was a child . . . She had men turning their heads to stare at her when she was twelve years old. She always knew she was going to be a beauty.

Mrs. Danvers (cont.)
They were a pair – her and her cousin, Mr. Jack . . . did just whatever they liked together. And she had the strength of a little lion. I remember her getting up on one of her father's horses – a real brute of an animal they said she'd never ride. I can see her now, her hair flying out behind her, slashing at him, digging the spurs in . . . she rode him, all right. She had him trembling all over – all froth and blood. 'That'll teach him, won't it, Danny?' she said . . . And that's how she went at life till she died . . .

108

Suddenly she breaks down and leans against the wall for support.

> **Mrs. Danvers**
> She's dead . . . she's dead.

She sobs openly. DAPHNE is sickened but pitying.

> **Daphne**
> You're ill, Mrs. Danvers . . . You should rest . . .
> see a doctor . . .

MRS. DANVERS turns on her fiercely – the sobs spluttering into rage.

> **Mrs. Danvers**
> Leave me alone! What's it to <u>you</u> if I show my
> feelings? I'm not ashamed of them! I don't shut
> myself up in my room to cry like Mr. de
> Winter! Oh, yes! I used to hear him behind his
> locked door – like a trapped animal!

> **Daphne**
> You must stop this.

> **Mrs. Danvers**
> He was <u>mad</u> about her – like every man who
> ever looked at her once! . . .

DAPHNE sees in her mind a dream-like image of:

<u>INT. NIGHT. MANDERLEY. REBECCA'S BEDROOM.</u>

MAXIM, distressed, looking out of the window.

> **Mrs. Danvers** (V.O.)
> And he was so jealous – he still is!

INT. DAY. MANDERLEY. REBECCA'S BEDROOM.

Abruptly the image of MAXIM is gone.

Mrs. Danvers
That's why he won't let Mr. Jack come here.

DAPHNE shakes her head sharply, and half-turns – putting her hands over her ears.

Daphne
I won't listen . . .

MRS. DANVERS pulls her hands away.

Mrs. Danvers
It's no use, is it? You'll never get the better of her. Even if she's dead, she's still mistress here, she'll always be the real Mrs. de Winter. Why don't you leave Manderley to her?

MRS. DANVERS leans closer, whispering to Daphne, almost hypnotising.

Mrs. Danvers
He wants to be alone with her again. It's you that should be dead. Why don't you jump?

She opens the window.

Mrs. Danvers
It's easy. It wouldn't hurt. Jump and have done with it. Then you won't be unhappy any more.

They both look down at the ground below.

DAPHNE seems about to surrender – a listless, sleep-walker's look about her as MRS. DANVERS whispers in her ear.

Mrs. Danvers
Go on . . . don't be afraid. It's for the best.

Dramatically the spell is broken – by a crashing explosion from outside. DAPHNE comes alive with a bewildered stare at MRS. DANVERS.

Daphne
What is it – what's happened?

MRS. DANVERS'S voice is flat – an instant return to her normal icy control.

Mrs. Danvers
It's the rockets. There must be a ship down in the bay.

Maxim (V.O.)
(urgent, commanding)
Frith? She's fast on the reef! They'll have to get the crew off! I'm going back down to see if I can do anything!

Frith (V.O.)
Very good, sir.

Mrs. Danvers
When you see Mr. de Winter, Madam, tell him there'll be a hot meal ready for the men at any time.

She turns and makes unhurriedly for the door, without looking back. DAPHNE has a flat stare of incomprehension.

EXT. DAY. SEA.

Everyone is gathering on the beach. MAXIM comes running down and jumps in a rowing boat, setting out towards the wreck.

111

INT. DAY. MANDERLEY. HALL AND STAIRCASE.

DAPHNE is sat at the bottom of the stairs. Frith arrives with a brandy.

Daphne

Thank you, Frith. I hope you won't think me odd. I've been in a bit of a daze.

Frith

Would Madam perhaps like me to send for Clarice?

She shakes her head.

Frith

Perhaps you'd like to lie down?

Daphne

No, no. In a moment or two I'll go down to the cove. Everyone else seems to be there.

Frith

Yes indeed. Very good, Madam.

EXT. DAY. MANDERLEY. WOODS.

DAPHNE makes her way down through the woods.

EXT. DAY. SECOND COVE/WOODS.

ESTATE WORKERS and LOCALS are gathered in groups round the bay. The SEAMEN are being helped from their boat. DAPHNE joins CRAWLEY who is looking out to sea with binoculars.

Daphne

Is anyone hurt?

112

Crawley

Nothing serious. She'll not go down too fast. Lifeboat's here at last.

He hands the binoculars to DAPHNE and she focuses them on MAXIM.

Crawley

Got him?

Daphne

Got him.

Crawley

Maxim's always absolutely splendid about anything like this . . . Can't do enough.

Daphne

I'm sure.

Crawley

I'd better go and round up the troops. They seem to want to make a day of it. Shall you stay?

He takes his binoculars back.

Daphne

Yes.

He moves away up the path. Out in the bay the rescue continues.

EXT. DAY. MANDERLEY. SECOND COVE & SEA.

DAPHNE walks further on down and stumbles upon BEN who is sitting on the rocks watching the rescue.

Ben

She'll break up bit by bit . . . She'll not sink
like a stone like the little 'un. The fishes have
eaten her all up by now, ain't they?

Daphne

What do you mean, Ben?

BEN jerks a thumb back along the beach – a nervous grin.

Ben

Her . . . the other one. I looked in . . . She said
she'd have me put in the asylum . . .
  (he gives a scared little laugh)
She can't now, can she? The fishes have eaten
her . . .
  (a pleading little whine)
They have, haven't they?

Daphne
  (gently)
You've nothing to worry about, Ben.

DAPHNE turns and moves down towards the sea.

*The rowing boat has reached the beach and MAXIM steps
out of it into the water and moves up the beach towards
DAPHNE.*

Daphne

Will they be alright – the sailors on the wreck?

Maxim

Yes, no-one's much hurt, the lifeboat's taking
the rest of them on to the harbour – hospital
check-ups.

Daphne
(gently)

Are you alright?

Maxim

What?

Daphne

You look tired.

Maxim

I haven't slept . . . I just walked . . .

Daphne

All night?

He nods.

Daphne

Have you forgiven me . . . for last night . . . all I
said?

He takes her hands in his.

Maxim

Am I forgiven?

Daphne

Can we start all over again? . . .
    (slight pause)
Be truthful with each other? Please, Maxim . . .
I've grown up since last night. I'll never be a
child again.

Maxim

Won't you?

*The moment is broken by the loud metallic voice of the
HARBOUR MASTER calling through a loud-hailer.*

Harbour Master (V.O.)
Mr. de Winter, sir . . . I have to see you, sir . . .
This is the harbour master . . .

They both turn towards him.

Harbour Master
Repeat – I have to see you, Mr. de Winter . . .
matter of urgency.

Maxim
(muttering)
What the devil is all this about?

He takes DAPHNE's hands again.

Maxim
Look, it's my stretch of the coast . . . some red
tape or other.

He walks towards Crawley.

Maxim
Look after things, Frank.

Crawley
Yes of course.

*He sets off walking down the beach towards the HARBOUR
MASTER.*

Harbour Master
If I could have a quiet word with you please,
sir? I'm sorry about this, but this is rather a
delicate matter and it should remain between us
for the time being.

DAPHNE, sensing something is wrong, runs to join them.

116

Harbour Master

The last thing I want to do is cause you both
any pain or distress. It's hard on you that we
can't just let the past lie quiet . . . But I don't
see how we can, under the circumstances . . .
we sent a diver down and he found something
none of us expected . . . The little sailing boat
that belonged to the late Mrs. de Winter . . . But
that isn't all . . . There's a body in the cabin. No
flesh on it, of course. The water's seen to that
. . . I'm sorry, Mr. de Winter, but it's my duty to
tell you . . . and report it further, officially, of
course.

Maxim
(quiet)

Yes. Of course.

Daphne

Rebecca was supposed to be alone . . . But there
was someone with her all the time . . . and no-
one knew.

Harbour Master

So it appears, Madam.

Daphne

But . . . there was so much about it at the time
. . . in the papers . . . And no-one was reported
missing?

MAXIM goes to her side to stop her saying more.

Maxim

Not now.

117

Harbour Master

Questions to be asked and answered . . .
There'll be publicity, I'm afraid . . . an inquest,
of course.

Daphne
(gently)
Maxim, I'm so sorry . . . Must you put my
husband through this all over again?!

Harbour Master
I have to report that body.

EXT. DAY. MANDERLEY. WOODS.

Maxim
It's too late . . . We've lost our chance of
happiness.

He paces around.

Daphne
No.

Maxim
It's happened . . . the thing I always knew
would happen . . . always . . . when I remember
that look in her eyes before she died . . . She
knew this would happen . . . Rebecca knew
she'd win in the end.

Daphne
(sickening fear)
What are you telling me?

Maxim
It's Rebecca's body they found in the boat . . .

118

Daphne
(barely able to speak)
No.

Maxim
Look, the woman buried in the crypt is someone belonging nowhere . . . no name . . .
unclaimed . . . There . . . never was an accident.
Rebecca didn't drown . . . I killed her . . . I
killed her, in the cottage. I carried her body to
the boat, and sank it.

DAPHNE can't take it all in.

Maxim
Can you tell me you love me now? No . . . I'm
a fool even to ask it . . .

Distraught, he turns away from her, looking out to sea.

Maxim
Over . . . everything . . .

Daphne
Maxim . . . Look at me. Look at me. Maxim.

He forces himself to face her.

Daphne
(a pleading insistence)
We can't lose each other . . . I love you,
Maxim. What else is there?

*She reaches up to hug him and they kiss each other,
desperately.*

119

Maxim
(whisper)
Oh God, I love you . . . I love you.

They hold each other in a clinging, aching embrace.

END OF PART SIX

PART SEVEN

<u>INT. DAY. MANDERLEY. MAXIM & DAPHNE'S
BEDROOM.</u>

DAPHNE and MAXIM are lying in bed.

Maxim

I hated her . . . We never really loved each
other. I don't think she was ever capable of
love . . .

Daphne
(appalled disbelief)
All those years . . . all a pretence?

Maxim

When I married her I was told I was the
luckiest man in the world – wasn't she so
lovely, so accomplished, so amusing? I got the
truth five days after we were married. You
remember that day in the car, up above Monte
Carlo? You asked me if I'd been there before
. . . well she told me all about herself . . . the
affairs she'd had . . . the sort of men . . . plenty
of detail . . . and she didn't intend to change . . .

<u>FLASHBACK.</u>
<u>EXT. DAY. FRENCH RIVIERA. SPRING 1920. COAST
ROAD HIGH IN THE HILLS.</u>

*The same spot as before, only this time it's MAXIM and
REBECCA.*

Rebecca
(taunting)
Look, I'll make a bargain with you . . . Of
course I'll look after your precious Manderley
for you, Max. I'll make it the most famous
show-place in the country. They'll say we are
the happiest, luckiest, handsomest couple in all
England . . .

She laughs contemptuously.

Rebecca
Oh what a triumph . . . what a god-damn triumph we'll be, Max.
(she laughs again)
Oh what a leg-pull . . . what a wonderful,
marvellous joke! You'll go along with it, Max
. . . Of course you will . . . Anything for the
pride and honour of your good name – and
Manderley. Of course you will.

Maxim (V.O.)
(low, bleak)
She was right . . . I did.

INT. DAY. MANDERLEY. MAXIM & DAPHNE'S BEDROOM.

MAXIM and DAPHNE in bed.

Maxim
I was a coward . . . I just couldn't face the
humiliation.

Maxim
She was so clever. They all believed in her
down here – servants, friends, relations, none of

122

them knew how she despised them all. She'd
walk around some garden party, arm-in-arm
with me, a smile on her face like an angel –
then the next day she'd go scurrying back up to
London to that flat of hers, like some animal to
its hole in a ditch . . .

*DAPHNE puts a hand over to him and he clasps it to his
chest.*

Daphne
You don't have to tell me any more.

Maxim
Months, years, I accepted it – because of
Manderley. What she did in London didn't
touch me, because it didn't hurt Manderley, so I
told myself, and then she started bringing her
special friends down here. The midnight picnics
at the cottage . . . especially that cousin, Jack
Favell . . .
       (voice full of disgust)
I couldn't allow that . . . not here . . . not him
. . . I told her I'd kill him if I found him any-
where at Manderley and one night I came home
late . . . She'd gone up to London that morning
and I was surprised – she'd come back already
. . . Some of her things in the hall – I knew
where she'd be . . .

FLASHBACK.
EXT. NIGHT. MANDERLEY. WOODS. 1926.

MAXIM hurries through the trees towards the cottage.

123

Maxim (V.O.)

And he'd be there with her. I couldn't stand it
any longer – all the lies, deceit. I had to make it
stop! She could live in London with him – or
any of the other men if she wanted to but not
here, not at Manderley! She could go! It was
over! Finished!

FLASHBACK.
INT. NIGHT. SECOND COVE. COTTAGE. 1926.

*REBECCA is sitting by the fire in the cottage, smoking a
cigarette.*

Rebecca

Well, you're wrong, Max. Put the gun away. He
isn't here. No-one's here . . . And it isn't over,
Max. I'm not prepared to just . . . go.

He puts down the gun.

Maxim

I'm divorcing you.

Rebecca
(little laugh)
Haven't you thought how damned hard that
would be? Think of us in a court of law. We
have the model marriage, don't we Max?
Everyone knows that.

Maxim
(quivering)
I'll get proof!

124

Rebecca
(hard, sharp)
No you won't! Not a chance! We've both
played our parts too well. We're a loving
couple. We adore each other. Not a servant here
knows any different. Take Danny. Did anyone
ever have a more personal maid?

She leans down and stubs out a cigarette.

Rebecca
She'd swear anything for me in court.
(dismissively)
You wouldn't have a hope in hell.

Maxim
(quiet, cold rage)
I could kill you.

She stands to face him.

Rebecca
Suppose I had a child, Max . . .

Rebecca
Who's going to prove it isn't yours? No-one. It
would give you the thrill of your life, wouldn't
it Max, to watch my son grow into his
inheritance.

Maxim
It won't happen.

REBECCA laughs in his face.

Rebecca

God, it's so funny . . . All the smug locals, and
the miserable peasants who bow and scrape to
you – they'll be so pleased . . . 'What we've
always hoped for, Mrs. de Winter,' they'll all
say . . . I'll be the perfect mother, Max – just
like I've been the perfect wife. And none of
them will ever know!

*MAXIM can't stand it any more and launches at her, grab-
bing her round the throat, knocking her backwards.*

INT. NIGHT. MANDERLEY. MAXIM & DAPHNE'S
BEDROOM.

DAPHNE's reaction to MAXIM's story.

FLASHBACK.
INT. NIGHT. SECOND COVE. COTTAGE. 1926.

He strangles her until she is dead.

INT. NIGHT. MANDERLEY. MAXIM & DAPHNE'S
BEDROOM.

Maxim

I got her into the cabin – took the boat out into
the bay . . .

FLASHBACK.
EXT. NIGHT. THE BAY OFF SECOND COVE.

*MAXIM is on the deck of REBECCA's sailing boat – strug-
gling to stay upright as the boat plunges in the wind and
swell. He flings the iron spike away into the sea.*

126

Maxim (V.O.)

. . . and used a spike to drive holes in the
bottom boards. I left her there . . . I waited and
watched till it was all over . . . It seemed like a
lifetime.

*MAXIM sits at a safe distance, watching as the sailing boat
finally sinks.*

INT. DAY. MANDERLEY. MAXIM & DAPHNE'S BEDROOM.

MAXIM is standing at the window – smoking a cigarette.

Maxim
(quietly)

The boat sank too close in to the shore. I
couldn't handle her well enough . . . If I could
have got her right out beyond the reef, they'd
never have found her.

Daphne

It was the shipwreck . . . If that hadn't
happened . . .

Maxim
(simply)

She was too close in . . . And finding you hasn't
made any difference, has it? Loving you hasn't
altered things. She knew she'd destroy me in
the end.

Short silence.

Daphne

Rebecca is <u>dead</u>. She can't harm you any more.

DAPHNE goes to him – a sudden surge of strength. She puts both hands on his shoulders.

Maxim
But there's her body . . . They'll identify it . . . her rings, maybe some of her clothes. It's not like a body lost at sea, battered against the rocks.

Daphne
Well if they find out it's Rebecca, you must say that the other body was a mistake . . .
(even more insistent)
The body in the crypt was a mistake. When you identified it as her you were distraught, ill. You didn't know what you were doing. It was a mistake. You will say that, won't you, Maxim?

Maxim
(faint nod)
Yes, yes I will. I killed Rebecca. It's done . . . I don't have any remorse for that . . .
(more tenderly)
What I regret is what I've done to you . . . see, it's gone.

He tenderly touches her face.

Maxim
. . . that funny, young, lost look you used to have . . . that I loved so much. It's gone and it won't come back. I killed that too.

Daphne
(intense whisper)
But we have each other.

128

She puts her hand to his face.

Daphne
They can't prove anything against you. Nobody saw you that night. No-one knows but you and I, Maxim.

Maxim
. . . the only two people in the world. You must do this for us.

They kiss passionately.

<u>EXT. DAY. OPEN SEA.</u>

REBECCA's boat is dragged out of the sea.

<u>INT. DAY. KERRITH. CORONER'S COURT.</u>

MAXIM is in court giving evidence.

Coroner
You say it was nothing unusual for your late wife to take her boat out at night, entirely alone?

Maxim
Not at all unusual. It was one of her great pleasures in life.

Coroner
And she was an accomplished yachtswoman?

Maxim
Very.
(pause)
She was accomplished at everything she did.

Coroner
(testily)
I was asking specifically about her ability in the handling of a sailing boat.

Maxim
She was highly proficient.

Beatrice
(crossly)
What can it matter <u>now</u>? Stupid waste of time.

CORONER looks up sharply.

Coroner
I would prefer <u>no</u> comment on the evidence given in my court.

Giles
(softly)
Watch your step, girl.

Coroner
Sailing calls for caution in the judgement of weather conditions, doesn't it?

Maxim
Of course.

Coroner
Would you describe the late Mrs. de Winter as reckless?

Maxim
Certainly not.

Coroner
But she did have a reputation for welcoming danger?

Maxim

What do you mean?

Coroner

As a sportswoman, Mr. de Winter.

Maxim

Yes, I suppose that's true. She was not a timid person.

Beatrice

You can say that again.

Giles
(softly)

Manners, Bee.

They get a stern glare from the CORONER, before he turns back to MAXIM.

Coroner

A strong-willed woman, Mr. de Winter?

Maxim
(steadily)

It's fair to say she knew her own mind.

INT. DAY. KERRITH. CORONER'S COURT.

TABB, the boat builder, is now standing giving evidence.

Coroner

You are James Tabb, the boat builder and you say you carried out the work of converting the late Mrs. de Winter's sailing yacht from its original construction as a fishing boat of French design? Is that correct?

131

Tabb

It is, sir.

Coroner

Was the boat in a fit state to put to sea?

Tabb

She was, when I fitted her out in April last year.
It was Mrs. de Winter's fourth season with her.

Coroner

Had the boat ever been known to capsize
before?

Tabb

No, sir, and I'd have soon heard of it from Mrs.
de Winter if it had.

Coroner

I suppose great care would be needed to handle
this small vessel in rough weather?

Tabb

Well, she wasn't a cranky little craft like some
– she was stout and sea-worthy. Mrs. de Winter
had sailed her in much worse weather than
there was that night.

*DAPHNE, hearing the court door bang, looks around. She
sees MRS. DANVERS and FAVELL entering.*

Coroner

So did it surprise you that the boat was lost that
night?

Tabb
(emphatically)
I couldn't understand it and I've said so all
along!

132

Beatrice

Well she was lost – that's all there is to it!

Coroner

But surely, if Mrs. de Winter went below, probably for a coat as is supposed, and a sudden gust of wind came down from the headland, <u>that</u> would be enough to capsize the boat?

Tabb
(forcefully)

No, no – not in my view.

Coroner
(testily)

Well that seems to be what happened. No-one's blaming your workmanship. I accept your statement that you delivered the boat in sound condition, which is all I wish to know from you.

He then addresses the jury.

Coroner

It seems that Mrs. de Winter relaxed her watchfulness for a moment and lost her life. Such accidents have happened before in local waters.

Tabb
(firmly – not giving way)

Excuse me, sir – but there's a bit more to it than that.

Coroner
(sharply)

Indeed? What, precisely?

Tabb

After the boat was brought up I got permission
from the harbour master to examine her.
(pause)
What I want to know is – who drove the holes
in her planking?

A little buzz of excitement in the room.

Giles
(muttering)
What's the fellow telling us now?

Coroner

Are you saying – deliberately done?

Tabb

I am, sir.
(pause)
I'm saying the boat never capsized at all. She
was scuttled.

BEATRICE mutters angrily.

Beatrice

What does the man think he's saying?!

Coroner

Mr. de Winter, do you know anything about
these holes driven in the planking?

Maxim
(hard, dismissive)
Nothing whatever.

Coroner

It is a shock to you, of course.

MAXIM stands up and faces him.

134

Maxim

It was a shock to find that I made a mistake in identification some twelve months ago. Now I find that my late wife not only drowned in her cabin but that the boat was damaged with deliberate intent that it should sink! Does it surprise you that I am shocked?

Coroner (V.O.)

Mr. de Winter, we all feel deeply for you. But I have to inquire into this matter – and <u>will</u> do so. I don't do it for my own amusement.

Maxim
(harshly)

That's quite obvious.

Daphne
(whispers)

No Maxim – don't lose your temper.

Coroner

Do we agree that whoever took the boat out that night must have driven the holes in the planking?

Maxim
(coldly)

So it appears.

Coroner

It appears very strange, does it not?

Maxim

Certainly.

Coroner

You have no suggestion to offer?

Maxim

None at all.

Coroner
(pause)
Mr. de Winter, painful as it may be, it is my
duty to ask you a very personal question.

Maxim

Very well.

Coroner
Were relations between you and the late
Rebecca de Winter perfectly happy?

Outraged, BEATRICE stands.

Beatrice
That's disgraceful!

*DAPHNE slumps against GILES in a faint. MAXIM notices
immediately.*

Maxim
Will someone please help my wife?

Beatrice
We'll take her out.

*BEATRICE, GILES and CRAWLEY help DAPHNE out of
the court room.*

Giles
(muttering to Beatrice)
Let's get her out to the fresh air.

Beatrice
Poor girl.

Giles
Indeed. All right. Careful, careful.

END OF PART SEVEN

PART EIGHT

EXT. DAY. OUTSIDE CORONER'S COURT.

Outside they sit DAPHNE down and give her a glass of water to recover.

Giles

Feeling better? . . . Good girl.

DAPHNE manages a little smile back.

Daphne

Yes . . . I'm sorry . . . What a stupid thing to do . . . It was so hot in there.

Beatrice
(indignantly)

And that stupid little man asking those ridiculous questions! What does he think he's doing?!

Giles

Bloody silly business.

Daphne

Where's Maxim?

Crawley

He's still in there . . . They're probably going over all the evidence again . . . I'm going to take you home now.

Daphne
(agitated)

No – I have to stay with him.

Crawley

Maxim told me to take you home. Giles and
Beatrice will hang on here. It's what Maxim
wants.

Giles

And you'd better behave yourself in there, old
girl . . .
(grins)
Coroner ticked her off.

Beatrice

Stupid little man. Fancy listening to that boat
builder chap! How can he tell how those holes
were made after all this time?!

Giles

Bloody silly business.

Beatrice

Boat builder chap's probably a communist!
Making trouble. Just the sort of thing they do,
you know!

EXT/INT. DAY. COUNTRY ROAD APPROACHING
MANDERLEY.

CRAWLEY drives DAPHNE home.

Daphne

Jack Favell . . . why was he there?

Crawley

Rebecca was his cousin.

Daphne

Why was he there with Mrs. Danvers?

Crawley

He's known her since he was a boy.

Daphne

I know that, Frank! But what does he want
now! Is he going to tell them something?!
Something against Maxim?!

Crawley

(deflective)

I can't think what.

Daphne

Favell and Mrs. Danvers . . . so mixed up with
Rebecca . . . her other life . . . It frightens me.

Crawley

You need to lie down . . . All this has upset you.

She looks hard at him.

Daphne

You must know as much as anybody, Frank.
Tell me what you think's going to happen.

Crawley

As long as Maxim keeps his temper and doesn't
let the coroner rile him into saying things he
doesn't mean . . . why shouldn't it end up just
like it was before? . . . It always was a bit of a
puzzle . . . She was alone in the boat, and she
drowned . . . Strange accident.

Daphne

(quietly)

And that's all you know?

CRAWLEY doesn't answer.

<u>EXT. DAY. MANDERLEY. FRONT OF HOUSE.</u>

DAPHNE and CRAWLEY stand at the foot of the steps.

Crawley
You will lie down, won't you?

Daphne
I ought to be there with him . . .
> *(sudden surge of fear)*
. . . He will come home today, won't he?

Crawley
> *(gentle but firm)*
Please go and rest.

She reaches out to squeeze his arm, then starts up the steps. Distant thunder sounds.

<u>INT. DAY. MANDERLEY. MAXIM & DAPHNE'S BED-ROOM.</u>

DAPHNE lies on the bed in an uneasy sleep. A storm rages outside.

<u>DREAM SEQUENCE.</u>
<u>INT. DAY. ASSIZE COURT.</u>

She dreams of the CORONER's court, REBECCA's boat capsizing and then MRS. DANVERS trying to get her to jump out of the window.

Mrs. Danvers (V.O.)
Go on. Don't be afraid.

Her dream moves on to visions of MAXIM strangling REBECCA and then when MAXIM is about to be sentenced:

Maxim (V.O.)
(angry, defiant)
I'm glad I killed her! I'm glad I killed her!

A sudden huge clap of thunder wakes her.

INT. DAY. MANDERLEY. MAXIM & DAPHNE'S BEDROOM.

She sits up and looks at her watch and goes to the dressing table, and starts to brush her hair.

Maxim (V.O.)
You see it's gone . . . that funny, young, lost look you used to have that I loved so much . . . it's gone and it won't come back. I killed that too.

EXT. DAY. MANDERLEY. HOUSE. GARDEN.

DAPHNE comes running down the front steps into the rain – she hasn't bothered with a topcoat or umbrella. CRAWLEY's car pulls up and MAXIM gets out and goes to DAPHNE, taking her hands in his.

Maxim
The jury brought in suicide . . . without sufficient evidence to show state of mind.

Daphne
Finished . . .

Maxim
Not quite. Frank and I have to go to the church . . . to bury her . . . Just the two of us and the vicar . . . and then it's over. Go in.

He kisses her quickly.

142

Maxim

I have to go.

He turns abruptly and gets back into the car. DAPHNE stands in the rain, watching the car move off. In her mind she imagines the funeral.

INT. DAY. CHURCH. CRYPT.

In the half-light of the gloomy, stone-flagged burial cellar, REBECCA's plain coffin is being lowered into its dark hole.

INT. NIGHT. MANDERLEY. DRAWING ROOM.

DAPHNE sits having tea.

Daphne

Yes ... Please show him in, Frith.

Frith

Very good, Madam.

He turns and makes for the door and DAPHNE stands up to face FAVELL. FRITH has barely got out of the room before FAVELL comes in – mopping his damp face and hair with his handkerchief, speaking with his insolent, menacing familiarity.

Favell

Good of you to let me in out of the rain ... I
didn't think old Max would be back yet ...
Last rites and all that ...
> (easy smile)
I just brought old Danny back ... She's feeling
a bit knocked sideways by it all.

Daphne

What do you want?

Favell

Well at this precise moment I could do with a
large whiskey and soda . . . Mind if I help
myself?

*Before she can answer, he goes to the side table, and mixes
his drink. She sits down again.*

Daphne

Why do you want to see Maxim?

Favell

Oh you'd have been proud of old Max, if you'd
stayed . . . Terrific show he put up . . .
Stonewalled 'em all the way . . . Such dignity –
never raised his voice. Made that little ferret of
a coroner look a real guttersnipe with his prying
questions.

Daphne
(quickly)

What questions?

Favell
(unpleasant grin)

Oh, nothing damaging . . . although he would
keep fishing . . . Did Rebecca have any money
troubles, for one thing . . . money troubles, for
God's sake! Old Rebecca must be laughing her
knickers off!

Daphne

Wouldn't it be better if you called at the estate
office in the morning – if you need to see
Maxim?

Favell
(a pouting smile)
Oh, now, don't chase me away . . . You think
I'm the big bad wolf, don't you, but I'm not
really, I'm just a perfectly ordinary, harmless
bloke . . .

He leans against a chair.

Favell
And I think you're behaving splendidly over all
this. Taking on this great place. Meeting all
these people you've never seen the like of
before . . . putting up with old Max and his
moods . . . And then finding out the truth of it
all . . . Because you do know the truth, don't
you – just like I do? That's why you fainted at
the inquest, isn't it?

Daphne
(hurriedly)
I don't understand you. I think you should
leave.

He stands, menacing.

Favell
I'm going to see justice is done to Rebecca . . .
Suicide. My God! Where did they pick that jury
from – the local loony-bin?

*At that moment, MAXIM comes striding into the drawing
room, closely followed by CRAWLEY.*

Maxim
Out of this house, Favell – you've been told
before!

145

He holds out a hand to DAPHNE which she takes. FAVELL smiles and finishes his drink.

Favell

Hold on, Max – I'm here to congratulate you on the inquest . . . Raise a glass to your nerve . . .

His glass is empty and he gestures towards the drinks.

Favell

Oh do you mind if I? . . .

Maxim

Do you want to be thrown out?

FAVELL's manner is abruptly harsh, ugly.

Favell

Yes, you'd better listen to me, Max. I can make things very unpleasant for you – dangerous, in fact!

Maxim
(quiet, hard)

Tell me how.

FAVELL lightens his tone again – sweetly reasonable.

Favell

Well, now look, Max, let's come clean about all this . . . I don't suppose there are any secrets between you and your wife – and from the look of things Crawley here makes up a happy trio . . .

Maxim

Would you like to leave us alone?

Daphne

No . . . I'd rather stay . . . really, Maxim.

MAXIM leads her back to her chair and stands beside her.

Favell
(cheerily)

So. I'll speak plainly. You all know about
Rebecca and me. We were lovers. I've never
denied it – never will . . . When she drowned it
hit me hard . . . bloody hard . . . But it seemed
it was just an accident – just lousy bad luck . . .
until today. Now we know better. Nothing to do
with luck, was it, Max?

Crawley

Suicide. Legal verdict.

Favell
(harshly)

Except that I have other evidence.

*He sets his drink down and produces a single sheet of
notepaper from his inside pocket.*

Favell

This is the last letter Rebecca ever wrote to me.
It has a date and time on it . . . the afternoon
before she died. Listen,
(he reads)

'I tried to ring you from the flat, but could get
no answer. I'm going down to Manders right
away. I shall be at the cottage this evening, and
if you get this in time will you follow me down
in the car. I'll spend the night at the cottage,
and leave the door open for you. I've got something to <u>tell</u> you, and I want to see you as soon
as possible . . . Rebecca.'

147

Silence. The other three can't look at each other.

Favell
(quietly)

'I want to see you as soon as possible. . .' Is
that the sort of note you write when you're
about to commit suicide? 'I've got something to
tell you . . .' And then you drown yourself?
(pause)
Trouble was I'd been to a hell of a party that
night – didn't see the letter till the next morning. By the time I got round to phoning here old
Danny gave me the news.

He gives a sour little grin.

Favell
Didn't help the hangover much.

*He puts the letter back into his pocket and picks up his
drink.*

Favell
If I'd read this letter out to the coroner today
that would have made things a bit tricky for
you, wouldn't it, Max?

He drinks.

Maxim
(steely)

Why didn't you?

Favell
Well for one thing, old Danny doesn't know
about it yet . . .
(confidingly)
And I don't think we want her to, do we? I

148

mean if old Danny were to find out that someone else had smashed those holes in the boat –
that someone had murdered her beloved
Rebecca, and it was you Max, in a jealous rage,
which is what I'd certainly tell her . . .

Favell
Well, I'd say that'd send old Danny right off
her rocker – and God knows what she might be
capable of . . .
(smiles at them)
You and yours wouldn't be safe, Max, even if
you were to get away with it in court . . . which
I doubt, anyway.

*He drinks again. DAPHNE goes and takes MAXIM's hands
in hers.*

Daphne
Maxim.

Crawley
(firmly)
You're just guessing. You have no proof.

FAVELL's tone changes instantly – a sneering contempt.

Favell
Good old loyal Frank – always ready to suck up
to your lord and master.

Maxim
(hard, threatening)
Stop that, Favell! What is it you want?

FAVELL finds his pleasant tone again.

Favell

Oh look, I don't want to smash you Max. God
knows you've never been a friend to me, but I
don't bear any malice about that. All married
men with lovely wives are jealous, aren't they?
And some of them just can't help playing
Othello. I don't blame them – I'm sorry for
them . . .

Favell

I can't think why fellows can't share their
wives instead of killing them. What's the
difference. You still get your fun. A lovely
woman isn't like a motor tyre – she doesn't
wear out. No, the more you use her, the better
she goes.

Crawley
(angrily)

For God's sake, man!

Favell
(contemptuously)

You snotty little prig – you tried your luck with
Rebecca and didn't get very far, did you? Do
you think it'll be a bit easier with the new
bride? An arm every time she faints – and she'll
be so grateful, won't she?

*MAXIM leaps forward and smashes a fist into FAVELL's
face. FAVELL totters and crumples to the floor.*

Daphne

Maxim. No!

150

MAXIM hasn't finished. He bends down, grabs FAVELL by the lapels and drags him half-upright – ready to punch him again. CRAWLEY hurries forward to intervene as DAPHNE calls out urgently.

Crawley

Leave it. Leave it! You asked for that.

FAVELL goes to sit in a chair over the other side of the room, stemming his bloody nose with a handkerchief.

Favell
(sourly)

Did I? I want some money out of this, Max.

Maxim
(contemptuous dismissal)

For what?

Favell

Keeping quiet.

Maxim

Not a penny!

Crawley
(quietly)

What do you have in mind, Favell?

Favell

Two or three thousand a year – for life. You can afford it . . . Cheap enough to save your neck.

Maxim

Blackmail! Never!

Favell
(twisted grin)

Insurance – best you ever had.

151

Maxim

Frank – get him cleaned up, and get him out!

CRAWLEY puts a hand on FAVELL's arm to help him up – but FAVELL stands up, shrugging him off.

Favell

Max, it's all gone too far. Rebecca's note . . . the way you set about me – the jealous rage, just the way you <u>had</u> to kill Rebecca. If I go to the police they'll have to put you on the spot.

Maxim

No-one's going to arrest me just for giving you a bloody nose. It's an occupational hazard in your kind of life, isn't it?

Favell

Max, old boy, see sense. Make me an offer . . .
(much harder)
Or else.

Maxim
(curt, business-like)
While you're washing your face, Favell, I'm going to call Colonel Julyan – he's the district magistrate. When he gets here you can tell him your story – and see what he thinks about blackmail.

Favell
(startled)
You wouldn't dare!

Maxim

Frank, get him to the bathroom, please . . . Colonel Julyan can be here in half an hour.

152

*CRAWLEY tries to take FAVELL's arm again but FAVELL is
having none of it. FAVELL moves towards the door.*

Favell
Right, Max – you're putting a noose round your
neck!

Crawley
Come on, man – you're drunk.

Favell
You and your bride think about that! You had
your chance!

They both exit.

Daphne
He knows . . . he knows.

Maxim
I'm calling his bluff.

Daphne
He only wants money – you have money. You
could send him away.

Maxim
No. He'd always be there. We'd be his
prisoners – like I was Rebecca's.

Daphne
I'm so frightened, Maxim. I know something
dreadful will happen if we don't stop him.

Maxim
It's the only way – face him down, till he's got
nothing left and then we're finished with him
and finished with Rebecca. Remember – he's
only guessing. He knows nothing.

Daphne

Oh Maxim.

He strokes her face tenderly.

Maxim

I'm going to call Julyan.

He leaves the room.

EXT. NIGHT. MANDERLEY. DRIVE.

A car comes up the drive and pulls up in front of the house. COLONEL JULYAN gets out and goes to the door and a FOOTMAN lets him in.

INT. NIGHT. MANDERLEY. LIBRARY.

COLONEL JULYAN stands reading REBECCA's letter to FAVELL. Everyone else is seated except MAXIM who stands by DAPHNE. FAVELL is still steadily smoking and drinking.

Col. Julyan

Why haven't you spoken up about this before?

Maxim
(sharply)
Because he hoped I would pay him not to . . .
Preposterous! He's playing a confidence trick –
that's all.

Favell
(grimly)
And he's a murderer – and he'll pay for that.

154

Col. Julyan

Gentlemen, I am here because of serious accusations made by both of you. Not in order to witness a brawl.

(pause)

As for this letter, it isn't evidence of anything criminal.

Crawley

Precisely.

FAVELL takes the letter back.

Favell

There's more – what's behind it. Rebecca wasn't a wife to you – admit it. When was the last time she let you touch her? She was going to ditch you and marry me and you could see it coming, couldn't you, Max – the shame of it, the public degradation. Too much for Maxim de Winter – so you killed her.

Maxim

Utter make-believe.

Crawley

Who's going to say all this in court, apart from you?

Favell

Call in the police – I'm ready.

DAPHNE looks alarmed.

Col. Julyan
(calmly)
I hardly think you are . . . just yet.

FAVELL keeps drinking.

Crawley
Give it up, Favell – you don't have a single
witness.

Favell
Oh don't I? You could be wrong . . . There is
someone . . . He was always creeping about the
woods and the bay – and the cottage. He saw
plenty he shouldn't have seen. We had to scare
him off . . .

DAPHNE thinks back to her first meeting with BEN.

FLASHBACK.
EXT. DAY. MANDERLEY. SECOND COVE.

Ben
I never said nothing did I?

INT. NIGHT. MANDERLEY. LIBRARY.

Favell
Shall we have the sweet-smelling Ben along to
tell us what he saw when he was playing
Peeping Tom?

Daphne
(too quickly)

No, don't!

MAXIM puts a restraining hand on her shoulder.

Daphne
I mean it isn't fair on someone like that.

Favell
Max?

156

Maxim
Frank, would you be good enough to get Ben
along here please. It shouldn't take long.

CRAWLEY stands and makes immediately for the door.

Crawley
Yes, yes of course.

FAVELL lifts his glass to MAXIM.

Favell
(mockingly)
To Manderley – eh, Max? You did it all for this
pile of stones and a few serfs tugging their fore-
locks. Can I get anybody a drink?

He beams round at them and stands up.

INT. NIGHT. MANDERLEY. HALL.

*CRAWLEY with his hand on BEN's arm, gently ushers him
towards the library.*

Crawley
(gently)
Now don't worry, Ben . . . There's nothing
wrong . . . No-one is going to hurt you.

INT. NIGHT. MANDERLEY. LIBRARY.

BEN enters the library, looking like a frightened animal.

FAVELL advances slowly on him.

Favell
Hullo, Ben . . . How's life been treating you
since I saw you last?

BEN looks timidly back at him.

157

Favell
Come on, you know who I am, don't you?

Ben
(uncertainly)
Eh?

FAVELL produces his cigarette case and offers it to BEN.

Favell
Go on, take one . . . as many as you like.

BEN looks at CRAWLEY for reassurance.

Crawley
(gently)
It's all right, Ben.

BEN carefully takes two cigarettes.

Favell
(harder)
Now. You know me, don't you? You've seen me at the cottage on the beach – haven't you?

Ben
(mumbling, scared)
I never seen you.

Favell
(roughly)
Don't be a bloody fool! You saw me at the cottage with Mrs. de Winter!

Ben
(shakes his head)
I never seen you.

FAVELL angrily takes a couple of pound notes from his inside pocket and sticks them under BEN's nose.

Favell
Will this make you remember?

BEN is even more scared – looks past FAVELL.

Ben
Has he come to take me to the asylum?

Favell
Answer me! You saw me with Mrs. de Winter – more than once!

Ben
She's gone.

Favell
You saw us in the woods and at the cottage!

Ben
I never seen you.

Crawley
Don't be frightened, Ben.

Ben
I don't want to go to the asylum – I want to stay at home.

FAVELL grabs BEN by the lapels as if to hit him.

Col. Julyan
Favell!

Favell
Oh, yes – he's Manderley property! He says whatever you tell him! My God, he'd tell the truth if I put a stick across his back!

BEN has had enough and suddenly goes running for the door. CRAWLEY is about to go after him – but MAXIM swiftly takes charge.

Maxim

All right, Frank.

He strides hurriedly from the room.

INT. NIGHT. MANDERLEY. HALL.

MAXIM stands beside the whimpering BEN, giving instructions to ROBERT.

Maxim

Find him something nice to eat, Robert, and then take him home . . .
(gently)
Off with you, Ben . . . Nothing's wrong . . . Don't hurry him, Robert.

Robert
(stiffly)

Yes, sir.

BEN shuffles away with ROBERT.

INT. NIGHT. MANDERLEY. LIBRARY.

MAXIM speaks – hard, cold – as he comes into the room. Favell is helping himself to another drink.

Maxim

Get out, Favell!

Favell

Not finished yet.
(pause)
Get Danny in here . . . Let's tell her who killed Rebecca.

160

Maxim

Frank – do as he wishes.

FAVELL sits down again and gets out another cigarette.

Favell

How did you do it, Max? You didn't beat her
brains in . . . no sign of violent injury. Did you
uh . . . smother her? Strangle her? Drown her?

Col. Julyan
(sharply)
Don't over-reach yourself, Favell.

Immediately, the sound of the door opening.

Maxim

Mrs. Danvers, please come in.

*MRS. DANVERS walks to the middle of the room, facing
them, and CRAWLEY re-joins them.*

Maxim

Mr. Favell has something he wants to ask you.

Favell

Right, Danny, tell these people about Rebecca
and me.

Mrs. Danvers
(pause)
Tell them what?

Favell
(sudden impatience)
You know damn well! We lived together on and
off for years, didn't we? She was in love with
me, just tell them!

Short silence, before MRS. DANVERS looks straight at him – her voice harsh, scornful.

Mrs. Danvers

No she wasn't. She wasn't in love with you or Mr. de Winter or any man! She despised all men! She was above all that!

Favell

You old fool! Didn't she meet me night after night at the cottage?! Didn't we spend the weekends together in London?!

Mrs. Danvers

(biting contempt)

What if she did?! She had a right to amuse herself, hadn't she?! Love?! With you?! With any of you?! It was a game to her!

Mrs. Danvers

She told me so! Make love with you?! Or any man! She did it because it made her laugh! I've known her come back and sit upstairs in her bed and shake with laughter at the lot of you!

She is losing her control, half-laughing, half-crying.

Mrs. Danvers

You were her favourite . . . but it was always a game . . . I was the only one she really loved.

She weeps quietly to herself.

Mrs. Danvers

They say that drowning is painless . . . isn't it?

The men all look embarrassed. DAPHNE stands and goes quickly to her. MRS. DANVERS allows herself to be led to a chair well away from the MEN.

Crawley
(quietly)
There's your witness, Favell.

Favell
There's still Rebecca's letter – it was no suicide note. She was going to tell me something . . . What, for God's sake? If we knew that it might explain everything . . .

Crawley
Well you'll never know now.

Favell
It might just tell us what it was made you snap at last . . . eh, Max?

Crawley
You're finished – you're clutching at straws.

Favell
I didn't know she was in London that day. What was she doing? Who did she see?

Crawley
Pointless – forget it.

Maxim
(steadily)
No, Frank – let him chase his own tail, if he wants to. It's something dogs do.

Favell
I'm going to nail you, Max, one way or another.

Col. Julyan
No, you're not Favell. Not without evidence
and we don't know where she went that day.

MRS. DANVERS suddenly speaks from across the room, composed again.

Mrs. Danvers
I have her private engagement diary. I kept all
those things. Mr. de Winter never asked for
them. There's an address book too. Do you
want to see them?

Favell
(grateful smile)
Thank you, Danny.

Col. Julyan
Uh . . . de Winter do you mind if we see this
diary?

MAXIM gestures that he doesn't mind.

Favell
Well shall we go and get it?

FAVELL stubs out his cigarette.

Col. Julyan
I think I should do that . . . Mrs. de Winter will
you come with us?

Daphne
Of course.

The three of them exit.

Favell
Now where will this lead us, Max?

He takes a gulp of whiskey and smiles.

END OF PART EIGHT

PART NINE

INT. NIGHT. MANDERLEY. LIBRARY.

COLONEL JULYAN is in the far corner, murmuring into the phone. DAPHNE talks quietly to MAXIM in the other corner.

Col. Julyan

Yes, if you would, please. It is rather important.
Well, that would be splendid . . . yes.

Daphne

She went to her hairdresser, then to her club for
lunch – and then to see someone called Baker . . .

They look up as he speaks more loudly into the phone.

Col. Julyan

Thank you very much . . . Most considerate.
Goodbye.

He replaces the receiver, walks steadily towards them.

Col. Julyan

Baker is a medical man – clinical consultant,
women's specialist. He'll see us tomorrow
afternoon.

Favell

And you know what he's going to say don't
you, Max? Now it all fits together. Now we
know what sent you over the edge that night.
Rebecca was pregnant – with my child. She
told you, didn't she – just as she'd have told me
if I'd got down here. That drove you to frenzy
and you had to kill her.

166

DAPHNE's nerve goes and she claps both hands over her ears. MAXIM puts his arms around her to comfort her.

Daphne
(weeping)

Stop it! Stop it!

Maxim

How low can you stoop Favell?

Favell

You're finished, Max . . . I'm going to hang you.

He laughs.

EXT. NIGHT. MANDERLEY. SEA.

The pounding sea.

INT. NIGHT. MANDERLEY. MAXIM & DAPHNE'S BEDROOM.

DAPHNE and MAXIM in bed. DAPHNE observes MAXIM's anxious abstracted stare. She whispers.

Daphne

Maxim. Look at me . . .

MAXIM turns his head. He clasps her hand to his chest.

EXT/INT. DAY. COUNTRY ROAD FROM MANDERLEY.

MAXIM and DAPHNE drive together with FAVELL and COLONEL JULYAN following.

EXT. DAY. LONDON CLINIC. SUBURBAN STREET.

They arrive in London.

INT. DAY. LONDON CLINIC. DR. BAKER'S CONSULTING ROOM.

Dr. Baker
(quiet, calm)

The woman who consulted me, giving her name as Mrs. Rebecca Danvers, was very ill . . . very seriously ill.

Dr. Baker

Clearly she gave me a false name because she wanted confidentiality . . . and, you know, our profession has to respect that like the confessional.
(faint pause)
But from your description this was your wife, Mr. de Winter, and she's now dead . . . The circumstances are exceptional.

Favell
(sharply)

Yes, get on with it, can't you!

Slight pause as DR. BAKER looks at each of them, and then fixes his eyes on MAXIM.

Dr. Baker

There were two consultations. The second was to tell her the results of the examination and X-rays from the first . . . and their implications. She told me very forcefully that she wanted the plain and simple truth – no hints or evasions . . .

Maxim
(softly)

Yes . . . yes.

168

Dr. Baker

So that was what I gave her.
(slight pause)
She had no more than a few months to live . . .

Shock and pain on their tense faces.

Dr. Baker

The cancer had too firm a hold. An operation
would have been quite useless.

Dr. Baker

Outwardly she appeared to be a completely
healthy woman . . . But the pain would increase
from week to week and she would have to be
kept under morphia until the end came. She
said she'd been suspecting it for some time.

Favell
(a sickened mutter)
Oh, Christ.

Dr. Baker

There is one other thing I think you ought to
know, Mr. de Winter . . . The X-rays showed a
certain malformation of the uterus . . . which
meant she would never have been able to have
a child. But that was a quite separate condition
– nothing to do with the cancer.

Silence until MAXIM murmurs courteously.

Maxim

Hmmm . . . thank you for your assistance,
Doctor Baker.

169

<u>EXT. DAY. LONDON CLINIC.</u>

They walk towards the cars. Everyone is shocked.

Favell

Oh my God . . . Rebecca.

He pulls out a hip flask and takes a drink.

Favell

Tell that bloody fellow with the barrel organ to clear out. I can't stand his blasted row.

Maxim
(flatly)

Can he drive his car?

Favell

Just give me a minute. I'll be all right. This has been a damned unholy shock to me. Cancer. Who'd have thought a woman like that . . .

Colonel Julyan

Oh, pull yourself together, man, for heaven's sake.

FAVELL rallies.

Favell

Turned out well for you, eh Max. Your lucky day. You've got your motive for suicide – except I still don't believe it.

Col. Julyan
(firmly)

You'll have to now.

Favell

Not me.

Col. Julyan

Then you'll keep it to yourself. The law is most
severe on slanderous accusations. You two need
to be alone. I'll take Favell back to his flat and
catch the night train back . . .

(curtly to Favell)

Get in, Favell. This <u>should</u> be the end of the
matter . . . But you know how stories spread in
country districts – give people half a chance.
You might feel like getting away for a while.
Why not go abroad? Well. You know the old
saying – out of sight, out of mind. Just a
thought.

Daphne

Thank you.

He gives them a quick smile – then goes to the car.

FAVELL rallies enough to call out to them – mockingly.

Favell

Fare you well.

The car moves off.

<u>EXT/INT. NIGHT. MAIN ROAD TO WEST COUNTRY.</u>

MAXIM and DAPHNE travel towards Manderley.

Maxim

She lied to me about the baby – because she
wanted me to kill her.

(pause)

Her last practical joke. The biggest of them all.

DAPHNE places her hand over his on the steering wheel.

Daphne
(gently)
She can't hurt us any more.

Maxim
No.

Daphne
(slight pause)
Do you think Colonel Julyan could have
suspected?

Maxim
Quite possibly.

Daphne
And Frank guessed some time ago, didn't he?

Maxim
Oh I think so.

Daphne
But he'd never say anything.

Maxim
It's over. We've got to begin again.

INT. NIGHT. LONDON. FAVELL'S FLAT.

*FAVELL, dishevelled and blotchy with drink, sips at his
glass – brooding, malevolent.*

EXT/INT. NIGHT. WEST COUNTRY. MOORLAND
ROAD.

*MAXIM's car speeding along – no other traffic. DAPHNE
is asleep against his shoulder.*

INT. NIGHT. LONDON. FAVELL'S FLAT.

FAVELL, in the same position as before, takes a gulp at his glass and bangs it down on the table. He has made a decision and reaches out for the telephone.

EXT/INT. NIGHT. WEST COUNTRY. MOORLAND ROAD.

They travel on through the night.

INT. NIGHT. MANDERLEY. MRS. DANVERS' ROOM.

MRS. DANVERS holds a telephone receiver to her ear. Slowly she replaces the receiver, her face expressionless.

EXT/INT. NIGHT. WEST COUNTRY. MOORLAND ROAD.

DAPHNE is still sleeping, lost in a dream.

DREAM SEQUENCE.

DAPHNE imagines that MRS. DANVERS, bearing a lighted candle, is coming towards her.

INT/EXT. NIGHT. WEST COUNTRY. MOORLAND ROAD.

As she wakes, DAPHNE speaks just audibly.

Daphne
Where will we go?

INT. NIGHT. MANDERLEY. MAXIM & DAPHNE'S BEDROOM.

MRS. DANVERS with a lighted candle is moving around their bedroom, setting it on fire.

INT/EXT. NIGHT. WEST COUNTRY. MOORLAND ROAD.

MAXIM and DAPHNE still travelling.

173

INT. NIGHT. MANDERLEY. REBECCA'S BEDROOM.

MRS. DANVERS is now in REBECCA's bedroom, setting that on fire as well. Satisfied, she lies down on the bed, lovingly caressing REBECCA's nightdress.

EXT/INT. NIGHT. COUNTRY ROAD APPROACHING MANDERLEY.

MAXIM's car approaches Manderley.

> **Maxim**
> *(loudly)*

Christ!

DAPHNE comes out of her sleep – mild confusion.

> **Daphne**
What time is it? . . . The sky's so red . . . Is it dawn already?

> **Maxim**
> *(grim, thick-voiced)*
It's not dawn . . . it's Manderley.

EXT. NIGHT. MANDERLEY. HOUSE WITH FRONT GARDEN.

The great house – flames are shooting through its roof and upper windows; great billows of smoke.

There is a frantic urgency as SERVANTS, ESTATE WORKERS and FIREMEN from a rudimentary fire engine try to get hoses trained on the flames.

INT. NIGHT. MANDERLEY. REBECCA'S BEDROOM.

MRS. DANVERS has passed out from the smoke.

EXT. NIGHT. MANDERLEY. HOUSE WITH FRONT GARDEN.

Some of the SERVANTS are standing completely shocked.

MAXIM's car draws closer.

INT/EXT. NIGHT. MANDERLEY. MAXIM'S CAR.

MAXIM and DAPHNE look at each other in horrified silence as they approach the house.

EXT. NIGHT. MANDERLEY. HOUSE WITH FRONT GARDEN.

MAXIM pulls up and jumps out.

Maxim
Frank! . . . Frith! . . . For God's sake!

CRAWLEY and FRITH come hurrying to him from different directions.

Crawley
(urgently)
Don't get too close!

MAXIM is staring in agonised disbelief at the burning house.

Maxim
Can we save it?!

Crawley
Maybe the ground floor.

Maxim
My God . . . Manderley.

DAPHNE comes to join them all.

Frith
(quavering voice)
We saved what we could, sir.

Maxim
Is everyone out? Anyone hurt?

Frith
Nobody hurt, sir . . .

Crawley
(hard, flat)
No-one's seen Mrs. Danvers.

MAXIM begins to move toward the house.

Daphne
Maxim! Don't!

She clings to him.

Maxim
(harshly)
She may still be alive.

Daphne
(whispering)
Maybe she doesn't want to live.

Maxim
(tortured rage)
I won't let Rebecca kill her!

He tears himself away from her and starts racing to the house.

DAPHNE screams desperately after him.

Daphne
Maxim! Maxim!

INT. NIGHT. MANDERLEY. REBECCA'S BEDROOM.

MAXIM comes stumbling and retching through the smoke, as he fights his way into the room. He sees Mrs. Danvers slumped on the bed and lurches to her. She is barely conscious, so he lifts her on to his shoulder like a rolled carpet and staggers through the smoke and gathering flames back to the door.

INT. NIGHT. MANDERLEY. UPPER CORRIDOR AND GREAT STAIRCASE.

Through the smoke MAXIM appears with MRS. DANVERS over his shoulder, stumbling towards the head of the stairs. He starts down the stairs – but can manage only two or three steps before he loses his footing and he and MRS. DANVERS come rolling and twisting down the stairs – two helpless, broken bodies.

EXT. DAY. FRENCH RIVIERA. SPRING 1937.

Ten Years Later.

DAPHNE is back sketching the Riviera. Her voice is heard – quiet, wistful but without self-pity.

Daphne (V.O.)
Last night I dreamt I went to Manderley again
. . . The house was a tomb. Our suffering lay
buried in the ruins. There would be no resurrec-
tion. I knew that when I woke I would not be
bitter.

She picks up her things and goes to join MAXIM. She takes his arm and they walk back towards the house.

Daphne (cont.)

I would think of Manderley as it might have
been, if I could have lived there without fear. I
would remember the rose garden in summer,
tea under the chestnut tree, the murmur of the
sea from the lawns below. These things will
always be with me . . . Memories that can't hurt
. . . but we can never go back again. The things
we have tried to forget would stir again, and
that sense of fear, leading to blind, unreasoning
panic – now mercifully stilled, thank God –
might become a living companion, as it had
been before . . .

EXT. NIGHT. FRENCH RIVIERA. HOUSE WITH
BALCONY.

*DAPHNE comes out to join MAXIM who is sitting on the
balcony reading. She is still holding her sketch pad
although her attention is centred on MAXIM.*

Daphne (V.O.)

No, the devil doesn't ride us any more.
Happiness? It isn't a possession to be prized,
it's a state of mind. Both of us are free,
although not unscathed, of course . . . There
will never be children. But we are together, in
unison, with no barrier between us. He is
wonderfully patient, and never complains – not
even when he remembers . . . which happens, I
think, more often than he likes me to know.

THE END

Rebecca, The Official TV Tie-In, written by Geoff Tibballs, is also published by Chameleon Books.

This official book gives not only a fascinating behind the scenes look at the making of the television adaptation of Daphne du Maurier's classic, but also an insight into her life and the inspiration behind *Rebecca*.